MOVING IN CIRCLES
Underdevelopment and the Narrative of Uncertainty in the Global Periphery

Ignasio Malizani Jimu

Langaa Research & Publishing CIG
Mankon, Bamenda

Publisher:
Langaa RPCIG
Langaa Research & Publishing Common Initiative Group
P.O. Box 902 Mankon
Bamenda
North West Region
Cameroon
Langaagrp@gmail.com
www.langaa-rpcig.net

Distributed in and outside N. America by African Books Collective
orders@africanbookscollective.com
www.africanbookscollective.com

ISBN: 9956-763-26-8

© Ignasio Malizani Jimu 2016

All rights reserved.
No part of this book may be reproduced or transmitted in any form or by
any means, mechanical or electronic, including photocopying and
recording, or be stored in any information storage or retrieval system,
without written permission from the publisher

To my teachers and students

Table of Contents

About this book...x
Acknowledgements...xii
Abbreviations and Acronyms.................................. xiv

Chapter One: Introduction................................... 1
Idiom of moving in circles.......................................1
Narrative of uncertain socioeconomic development........6
Outline of the chapters..9

Chapter Two: Malawi: A contextual analysis.............. 11
Territory and environmental context.........................11
Demographic context...13
Social and economic context.................................. 15
Development and its challenges........................... 17
Concluding reflections 27

**Chapter Three: The meaning and content
of development**... 31
The meaning of development..................................31
Development since the Second World War................. 32
Ideology and development.................................... 39
Development and global politics........................... 43
Development as a normative concept.......................45
Paths to development 47

v

Chapter Four: Space, Place and Urban Economic Informality..55

Space, place and informality.................................. 55

The informal economy...................................... 58

Context and approach...................................... 60

State – street vendors' relations 1960s to 2000s............. 62

Location rationality and economic rights.................... 68

Streets as fluid spaces of opportunity....................... 69

Street vending and poverty alleviation discourse............71

Attitudes and prejudices against street vending............. 73

Reorganizing vending......................................74

Closing reflections...76

Chapter Five: Agriculture and the development impasse.. 81

Development as agricultural related crisis................... 81

Agrarian situation of Malawi................................ 86

Looking into the future..................................... 95

Prices, markets and development........................... 96

Appropriate technology....................................105

Effects of commercialization of smallholder agriculture... 113

Concluding reflections....................................115

Chapter Six: Commodification of customary land relations in peri-urban villages.....................119

The changing value of land.................................. 119

Customary land in perspective............................. 122

Locating the peri-urban 125

Commodification of customary land as a process.......... 125

Shifting attitudes towards the selling of land.................126

vi

Impacts on agrarian way of life............................ 130

Chapter seven: Multitasking and livelihood Diversification..135
Multitasking as a norm... 135
Definitions and implications................................. 137
Non-farm economy and poverty 146
Non-agricultural employment in Malawi.....................148
Developmental potential of non-agricultural activities...... 166
Deagrarianisation and reagrarinisation....................... 169

Chapter Eight: Perspectives on gender and development...173
Gender and gender relations.................................. 173
Gender in development paradigms...........................175
Unequal relations, unequal outcomes....................... 178
Bases of gender inequality 188
Gender and rural non-agricultural activities.................. 191
Gender and the participatory development paradigm...... 193
Closing reflections...198

Chapter Nine: Moving in Circles........................... 205
Two steps forward and three steps backward.............. 205
Recollecting half-century of development rhetoric 207
Politics of economic liberalizations......................... 209
Liberalization of currency..................................... 215
Pseudo-democratic promise and clientele politics.......... 217
Epilogue...221

References... 229

vii

viii

About this book

Moving in Circles is a collection of chapters drawing on empirical and historical studies focusing on the challenges of development in a developing country. The title 'Moving in Circles' is an idiom for lack of progress despite investment of time and effort. Some of the indicators of this condition are first and foremost pervasive poverty, uncertainty, liquidation of productive assets such as land, and precarious livelihoods. Uncertainty stands out as a cost as it is also a catalyst for low investment in agriculture, low returns non-agricultural activities, inconsistent approach to planning and rule of law, irrational politicking, nepotism and corruption and more generally socio-economic backwardness. Development should in a broad sense entail meeting human needs, actualization of local and domestic potential and liberation from uncertainty. It is argued that in the long term, for 'development' talk to be meaningful, there is need for progressive transformation of underlying structures, improvement in productive capacity and general adherence to principles of good governance: openness and transparency, accountability and meaningful popular engagement.

Acknowledgements

Acknowledgements are due to my teachers at the University of Botswana (Prof. Francis B. Nyamnjoh, Dr Onalena D. Selolwane and Dr Monageng Mogalakwe, Prof. John Oucho, Prof. Thabo Fako, Prof. Maipose, Dr Godisang Mookodi, Mr Roy Love, Dr Rob Pattman and Prof. Michael Neocosmos), to Prof. Till Förster of the Ethnologische Seminar of the University of Basel (Switzerland) and my students at Mzuzu University. Many thanks to late Mr W.M.K. Mwafongo and his colleagues at the Department of Geography and Earth Sciences of the University of Malawi and to Dezie Trigu, Dr Golden Msilimba, Zamzam Kome, Dr Veit Alt, Dr Lucy Koecklin, Dr Divine Fuh, Dr Peter Lindenmann, Dr Kerstin Bauer, Dr Ephrem Tesema, Dr Henri Yere, Dr Andrea Kaufmann, Dr Kathrin Heizt, Dr Fiona Siegenthaler, and Dr Bettina Frei, Andrea Poelling, Nina Schild, Keila Selafim, Nellie, Mahala and Luntha.

I share the merits of this book with reviewers unknown to me, the copy editors and the publisher who devoted significant amounts of time; moving in circles for over 15 months, commenting on and perfecting the manuscript.

IMJ
Lilongwe, Malawi

xii

Abbreviations and Acronyms

ADMARC	Agricultural Development and Marketing Corporation
AIDS	Acquired Immunodeficiency Syndrome
BMC	Botswana Meat Commission
DFID	Department for International Development (UK)
GAD	Gender and Development
GDP	Gross Domestic Product
GNP	Gross National product
HIV	Human Immuno-deficiency Virus
IMF	International Monetary Fund
IRDP	Integrated Rural Development Programme
LADDER	Livelihoods and Diversification Directions Explored by Research
MASAF	Malawi Social Action Fund
MDGs	Millennium Development Goals
MDHS	Malawi Demographic and Health Survey
MEJN	Malawi Economic Justice Network
MNCs	Multinational Corporations
PEP	Politically Exposed Person
PWP	Public Works Programme
TIP	Targeted Input Subsidy
TNCs	Transnational Corporations
UNDP	United Nations Development Programme
USAID	United States Agency for International Development

xiv

Chapter One

Introduction

Moving in circles

Moving in circles is an idiom for lack of progress notwithstanding investment of significant amounts of time and effort. Applied to development practice, therefore, moving in circles is a critique of decades of development practice in the global periphery, of which Malawi is a part. Investments of time, capital (both domestic and foreign), and effort are yet to begin yielding meaningful and sustainable gains, hence the timeliness of this investigation.

One of the development challenges for the global periphery is underdevelopment. Writing in the early 1970s on the difference between development and underdevelopment Walter Rodney argued that:

> Obviously, underdevelopment is not absence of development, because every people have developed in one way or another and to a greater or lesser extent. Underdevelopment makes sense only as a means of comparing levels of development. It is very much tied to the fact that human social development has been uneven and from a strictly economic view-point some human groups have advanced further by producing more and becoming more wealthy (Rodney 1973: 18 - 9).

Two central concerns critical to the underdevelopment thesis are comparative relations and exploitation. As Rodney put it, the moment that one group appears to be wealthier than others, some enquiry is bound to take place as to the reason for the emerging or growing socio-economic difference. Consequently underdevelopment is one of the roots of poverty in the global periphery. Its manifestations include the situation of being born into insecurities and uncertainties of various kinds – food insecurity, political, economic as well as environmental insecurity – and also dying surrounded by them. Hence, being uncertain means a being in a state of insecurity. The question to reflect on after several decades of development practice is whether the coming decades will lead to a different result.

Development and the desire for progressive change that it usually connotes are universal cravings across social, economic, political, spatial and temporal divides. To be precise, development implies change that is desirable, predictable and progressive and that leads to improvements in the means of production, income levels (in the form of profits, interests, wages and salaries), and employment rates. The sad reality is that change is not always progressive in orientation. Improvements in means of production as a result of capital intensive investments could increase productivity at the expense of jobs or exacerbate unemployment and a rise in income could magnify per capita income disparities; situations which could in turn lead to social and economic deterioration and sometimes social and political instability. Moreover, in the global periphery there is considerable craving for change even as there are fears that western-style development could be a catalyst for cultural erosion and economic inequality. Two questions therefore merit critical consideration at this juncture. These are: What is the nature of the status quo, and what could be ironical about it?

Beginning with the second question, what could be ironical about the status quo is the severity, depth and implications of inequalities that characterize and to some degree underlie unfolding social, economic and political relations. At the micro level, the inequalities are disguised without serious reflection as nothing but a characteristic feature of the limited capacity of respective societies in the global peripheral to shape their own futures. Lack of capacity to imagine and shape the future goes beyond parameters of choice and should be of concern in economic, political and human rights discourses. Take, for example, the lack of capacity anchored in the reality of unequal access to space in physical and metaphorical senses and the lack of opportunity and power to influence in a fundamental way the allocation of productive resources. Owing to underlying inequalities that are sometimes assumed to be part of the natural order, in numerous instances people on the lower rungs work very hard and for long hours in different economic sectors and yet earn very low returns in the form of income, satisfaction or quality of life.[1] Low-paying work can involve exploitation of workers by local, national, international and global systems.

Unequal and inadequate access to arable and range lands contributes to lack of and sometimes to diminishing of capacity. Inadequate access may be due to legal, institutional and cultural systems that either promote exploitation or celebrate marginalization and servitude within and between ethnic, regional, national communities and at international level. As Katar Singh once put it, 'As long as a society is bound by the servitude of men to nature, ignorance, other men, institutions, and dogmatic beliefs, it cannot claim to have achieved the goal of development' (Singh 1999:22).

Access to land and to subterranean minerals resources is a fundamental development dilemma, as is access to relatively mobile resources such as capital and technology, which ironically are neither infinitively mobile nor equally distributed. Addressing imbalances in the allocation of resources without reforming systems that buttress inequality, including those underlying patterns of international trade, would not address disparities. No wonder that inequality in any form reflects a state of underdevelopment. To understand the depth and implications of underdevelopment and consequently the moving in circles, there is need to understand how these phenomena arise and how they are maintained by forces operating at different spatial and political levels.

Within many developing countries, the lack of capacity to exploit resources within given territorial and political contexts, partly as a result of peculiar challenges of nature and lack of technical knowhow, is today one of the fundamental anchors of both low and uncertain levels of production and development. This is the reality of many resource rich and resource poor nations of the global periphery known also as the global south. Indicators of their peripheral condition include low productivity, underdevelopment of resources, poor infrastructure, low savings, and low investment, marginalization of rural populations, ever rising urban unemployment and urban poverty rates, and overall unhealthy dependency on the global north for capital, market and security.

The spatial and temporal importance of the discourse of poverty, inequality and dependency lies in its effects on socioeconomic reality. Both for the countries of the global south and the very poor people within these peripheral nations, the reality of being at the bottom influences how they ultimately perceive the world around them, how they go about exploiting resources at their disposal and also attribute meaning to events and challenges around them. In essence, and this is an empirical generalization, how human beings react to their reality reflects the meanings they assign to it, and their reality cannot be understood in any other way than through the prism of the social, economic and even political upheavals that shape their lives and underwrite their vulnerability.

Cycles of economic, political and social upheavals on the African continent and abroad are signs of precarious economic and social foundations. Yet precarity is not a state of stalemate. Sometimes the pace of change is so rapid, and uncertainty seems to increase at such a rate that effective adjustment is next to impossible. It becomes extremely worrying when there is a mismatch between assumptions and actions relative to the objective reality. Some of the regrettable effects are the reproduction of inequalities, conflicts over dwindling resources or power, and the eventual creation of permanent winners and losers. The last effect is not new and not strange given that the global political economy is structured to produce and reproduce inequality. That is, inequalities engineered at the global level get reflected at the national and local levels such that development talk and practice create inequalities of all kinds at different spatial scales. Ironically, there is a tendency to celebrate the ability of disadvantaged people to make rational and creative choices, to face adversity and overcome it; yet the same people are portrayed as hapless victims not responsible enough for their own actions (Wilk 1996). Such contradictions permeate the narrative of moving in circles and uncertain development.

Narrative of uncertain socioeconomic development

Writing on developmental states in Africa Nyamnjoh and Jimu (2005) observed that independence movements throughout sub-Saharan African gained popular following on the back of promises of freedom and socioeconomic development preceded by a century or more of slavery, colonial domination and underdevelopment. The idiom of moving in circles captures the disillusionment with the development promise and socio-economic alienation of the masses thereafter.

Since the dawn of independence in the 1960s and of multiparty politics in the mid-1990s, development talk has benefited to a meaningful extent a handful of individuals only. A majority of people live life rife with poverty, while a handful have in turn and in different ways, guises and at different times facilitated the direct and indirect appropriation of both the discourse and resources and filtered them to friends, associates, and members of their families. There is a lack of sufficient commitment and momentum to redirect the development discourse and practice through sound development strategies.

A sound development strategy unequivocally indicates who will take the main responsibility for expanding the economy, and hence gain from the programmes, projects, activities and more generally the accumulation of capital. It also suggests, explicitly or implicitly, which classes and strata will have to bear the major part of the burden of that socioeconomic change. Second, a development strategy prescribes how the economy should be run to achieve growth and other operative goals which may, for instance, include equity, mass welfare and national autonomy (Sandbrook 1982). Uncertainty over the development strategy or operative policy goals is recipe for slow to lack of progress and the narrative of uncertain development in the global periphery.

A narrative is a story, though not every story would suit the label narrative in the sense intended here. Narratives have a plot or storyline, a beginning, middle and ending. Narratives tell about social life, rules, norms and mores and are to that extent relational. Narratives also construct issues and persuade, leading the audience to read a specific situation in a particular way, and so they proliferate and legitimate ways of perceiving and analysing the world. As plain stories and scenarios, narratives can simplify ambiguity. It is thus important to appreciate the relational attributes, including the potential to moralize, generalize and even stereotype. Like all stereotypes, however, stereotypes in narratives can be wrong and therefore open to contestation. According to González (2003:77): 'The nature of what we believe is not only real but also the powerful determinant of all we see. Our relationship to what we know is equally influenced by the assumptions we hold about the nature of reality.' The challenge therefore is how to reconcile reality from imagination. Some careful thinking is needed to understand the ultimate place and importance of the idiom of moving in circles as it also relate to the narrative of uncertainty.

The first of the narratives regarding uncertain development could be under exploitation of development potential. For any nation to meet the development aspirations of its people by growing its economy there must be efficient utilization of resources. These may be land, labour, capital or technology required in various productive activities. A question to pose is: How can Malawi be poor while possessing relatively good agricultural land, relatively cheap labour and vast freshwater resources? Part of the answer is that Malawi has not developed aquaculture into an important contributor of economic growth and development. Nor have the country's leaders and businesspeople made significant strides towards harnessing abundant and relatively cheap labour force. The state of food insecurity is but a crisis of capacity and a reflection of lack of vision and political will, both domestic and international, as both are required to transform aquacultural and agricultural potential into food and cash crops, domestic and foreign exchange revenues, and raw materials and employment (self-employment and waged employment alike) on sustainable terms. Food insecurity stands out as an absurd ironical situation.

Other than the material realties of uncertain food supplies and uncertain prospects of employment, domestic and foreign commentators on the Malawi state have observed with regret the twists and turns since the early 1990s. Prior to the political transition, honesty and hardworking were important virtues. To date current and aspiring leaders as well as the working class seem to have short and circumscribed planning horizons. Those who contribute to uncertainty are unconvinced that their own actions and sometimes inaction are among the roots of impoverishment talked about. Other than feigning ignorance, they are not ready to conduct themselves differently or change tactics to propel a different outcome. Despite increased levels of awareness that in today's world nobody can live entirely on subsistence farming, regime after regime continues to subsidize farming for subsistence ends.

Another question worth posing is: What is required to achieve meaningful development? There are many answers to this question but most will revolve around addressing the indicators of lack of development and the uncertainty it leads to. Uncertainty occurs at different levels and invokes as it involves different sets of processes and relationships. In an economy characterized by low productivity and very wide disparities in wealth, any effort toward redistribution will not produce prosperity but an evening-out of poverty. The poor may become complacent, especially when redistribution involves gifts of assets that are nothing but empty symbols of affluence. The long term impact becomes a gross mismatch between people's real state and the borrowed success.

Outline of the chapters

This book is a collection of chapters drawing on empirical and historical studies. Collectively, the chapters reflect on the development impasse in Malawi and more generally in sub-Saharan Africa. The second chapter focuses on demographic and economic questions, thus providing background information for Malawi regarding the uncertainties to be reflected upon in subsequent chapters. Chapter three explores the meaning of development, approaches and disagreements on its content and direction. Chapter four examines street vending, an example of insecure urban livelihoods, and street vendors' relations with the state. Chapter five turns to agrarian transformation, challenges besetting smallholder agriculture and requirements for progressive transformation. Chapter six delves into uncertainties driving peri-urban land transactions; including changes in attitudes and practices, and how sellers and buyers negotiate and attribute exchangeability or interchangeability between land and money. It also addresses uncertain and precarious socioeconomic position of land sellers and the consequences of loss of access to land on livelihood security. Chapter seven explores multitasking, particularly the growing prominence of diversification into non-farm and non-agricultural activities, as well as its benefits and challenges. Chapter eight turns to relations between women and men in the spheres of production and social relations in the sphere of community participation. Such relations are unequally constructed and often result in social inequalities. The need for inclusion is reflected upon. The ninth and last chapter explores uncertainty by turning to the convergence of local and global realities.

Notes

[1] Even in the major industrialized economies of the world the need for improved quality of life is a major social concern. In the USA fast food workers and drivers make peanuts while the managers become rich.

Chapter Two

Malawi: A contextual analysis

This chapter introduces the territorial, environmental, demographic and socioeconomic circumstances of Malawi. The intention is to provide a background context for the later chapters covering the rise and place of the urban informal economy, smallholder agriculture and land tenure transformations in peri-urban villages and livelihoods diversification.

Territory and environmental context

Malawi, also known as Nyasaland during colonial times, is located in southern Africa.[1] Her territory stretches over 118 484 km^2 of which 94 276 km^2 is land mass[2] and the rest water. The major water bodies are Lake Malawi,[3] Lake Chilwa, Lake Malombe, and Lake Chiuta and the following major rivers: Shire, Songwe, North and South Rukuru, Bua, Mwanza, Linthipe, and Ruo. Shape-wise, Malawi is long but narrow (840 km long and varying from 80 to 160 kilometres in width).

Altitude or height above sea level varies greatly from 50 m in the Lower Shire in the South to 2600 m above sea level on the Nyika Plateau in the North, but the highest point lies more than 3000 m above sea level on the Sapitwa Peak on Mulanje mountain in the Southeast (Msilimba 2007). Other high-lying areas include Zomba Plateau (2100 m) in the South and Dedza Plateau in the Central Region. Lake Malawi and the Shire River are situated on the floor of the East African Great Rift Valley.

11

The climate in Malawi is subtropical with three seasons: hot-wet (November to April), cool-dry (May to August), and hot-dry (September to November). The rainy season extends from November to April, and the dry season from May to October. Temperatures vary from freezing at high altitudes to 38^0C in the lowest altitude. Notwithstanding the effects of climate change and variability, only one-third of Malawi has a mean annual rainfall in excess of 1000 mm; and five % of the country receives less than 750 mm of rain (Msilimba 2007). Variations in relief and topography exert considerable influence on temperatures and rainfall. In good years the high plateau areas could experience up to 2000 mm of rain, the medium plateau areas 900 to 1300 mm while the northern and southern lakeshore areas, the Shire Valley, and the middle (Kasungu and Mzimba) plains are relatively dry with less than 900 mm of rain. The wide range of altitude and climactic conditions allow the growing of tropical and subtropical crops.[4] Recently, climate change has become a matter of concern affecting Malawi's agricultural activities through cycles of drought and floods, short growing seasons and increased uncertainty. Climate change and global warming it is linked to, are associated with atmospheric concentrations of both carbon dioxide and methane, affecting basic climatic components of temperature and precipitation (Kerski and Ross 2005). A proportion of the increase is a consequence of deforestation, especially of tropic forests.[5] Due to erratic rainfall, coupled with declining soil fertility and growing pressure on land, many rural dwellers face increasing livelihood insecurity that includes food scarcity. Recently, deforestation has been closely tied to demographic, low socio-economic status of the population and the political situation; especially the discourse on human rights and political liberalization.

Demographic context

Malawi's population is growing steadily at a rate of 2.9% per annum (Government of Malawi 2010). The population grew from 737 000 people in 1901 to 13 million in 2008. However, at the end of World War II, the total population was 2 million people, of which 99.8% were Africans (Mitchell 1968). The first population census held in 1966, two years after attaining independence, reported 4 million people, representing a 97% increase over a period of just 21 years. The estimated population in 2015 was over 15 million people. With a doubling period of just over 20 years the population would grow to 30 million by 2035. The average population density has also risen from 43 persons per km^2 in 1966 to 139 persons per km^2 in 2008, representing an almost threefold increase over a period of 30 years. In parts of the Southern Region, population density ranges from 300 to 400 persons per square kilometre.

Over time there has been a slow demographic shift from the southern part of the country. At the time of independence over 50% of the population lived in the Southern Region, but the percentage has fallen to 45%, while the central and northern regions have experienced population increases. Countrywide the fertility rate is about 6.5 children per woman. The dependency ratio is high with about 11% of the adult population between the ages of 15 and 49 years outside the labour force. High HIV/AIDS infection rates contribute to the high dependency ratio.[6]

The 2004/05 integrated household survey estimated a mean household size of 4.5 persons per household across Malawi (Government of Malawi 2005) and the size was roughly the same in the 2008 population and housing census. Household size in rural areas was 4.6 persons, while that in urban areas was 4.3 persons per household. About 77% of households were headed by males and 23% by females. Of the male-headed households, the majority of the male heads (34%) were in the 25-34 age groups, and the least in the age group of 65 and over. Of the female-headed households, the highest number of female heads (26%) was in the age groups 50-64 and the lowest (9%) in the age group 10-24. These figures suggest that the rate of female-headed households increases in relation to the age of the head of the household.

The challenges being experienced by households include the burden of caring for orphans associated with mortalities from HIV/AIDS. HIV/AIDS continues to take a heavy toll on both rural and urban populations. For rural subsistence producers the impacts include reduced time for preparing, tending and harvesting crops and livestock and diminished skill acquisition by orphaned children. *The Economist* (2004:13 as cited in Nyamnjoh 2005:296-7) projected the view that 'All of Africa's famines are now AIDS-related: hungry people lack the strength to fight off sickness, sick people lack the strength to grow food, and dead parents cannot teach their children how to farm.' Low levels of education too restrict the capacity of many people to take full advantage of alternative occupational opportunities, and the incidence of chronic ill-health due to poor access to and affordability of health services reduces overall labour productivity.

Social and economic context

Malawi is a developing country. Common characteristics of developing countries, according to Szirmai (2005) and others, include widespread poverty and malnutrition, relatively large share of agriculture in output and employment, pronounced dualism in economic structure, very rapid growth population, explosive urbanization, large-scale underutilization of labour, political instability, pervasive corruption, environmental degradation including deforestation, siltation of water bodies, overfishing and depletion of soils, and low levels of technological capabilities connected to the challenge of inadequate schooling, training and experience.

At one time the poverty level in Malawi was pegged at 60%. To be precise, 60% was the poverty rate in the early 1990s, but by the end of the 1990s the rate went up to 65.3% (Government of Malawi 1995, 2000). Poverty, like development, is multidimensional. A report titled 'Consultation with the Poor' commissioned by the World Bank revealed that the poor in Malawi consider high prices of commodities, poor or reduced harvests, diseases, rise in death rates, unemployment and illiteracy as the common causes of poverty. Most participants indicated that poverty leads to malnutrition, a lot of debts, worries, thefts and murders, dependency on casual labour, hunger and illiteracy (Khaila et al. 1999). An integrated household survey of 2004/05 showed that about 52.4% of the population lived below the poverty line, with 22.4% barely surviving (NSO 2005). Using the United Nations Development Programmes' (UNDP) human development index (HDI), which focuses on income, literacy and life expectancy, only 12 of all 174 countries reporting in 2004 were below Malawi in terms of their HDI, and six of these countries were recovering from conflict or categorized as failed states.[7] For 2015, Malawi's was rated 173 out of 188 countries with HDI of 0.445, while the Sub-Saharan average was 0.518.

Economic figures for the past few years suggest a decline of extreme poverty. Malawi was hailed as an African success story when its GDP grew at an average rate of 6.8% per annum between 2004 and 2010 and the poverty rate declined from 52 to 39% (Mussa and Pauw 2011). Then it was reported that there were significant reductions in poverty in both rural and urban areas, with urban poverty falling from 25 to 14% between 2004 and 2009, and rural poverty from 56 to 43% over the same period. Even with such impressive economic growth, poverty persists and is characterized by persistent food insecurity, poor access to public goods and services.

The health sector is one of the critical areas. Malawi has the worst health worker to population ratio in the world with two doctors and 59 nurses for every 100,000 people (Department for International Development 2007). Health indicators at the end of the 1990s showed that life expectancy at birth dropped from 43 years in 1996 to 39 years in 2000. Recently there have been some improvements. Life expectancy was 61 years in 2013; and real income per capita was US$250 in 2014.[8] In 2000, the maternal mortality rate was 1,120 deaths per 100,000 live births, a rise from 620 in 1990. The 2004 MDHS reported a maternal mortality rate of 984 per 100,000 live births, while that of 2010 reported a rate of 675 maternal deaths per 100,000. Recent figures, as reported by the state through the public media, indicate a drastic drop of the maternal mortality rate to 460. There is need for independent verification since there is a strong temptation to falsify achievements.

For the poorest people, poverty often means hunger or vulnerability to food insecurity and lack of access to social services such as health care and education. Those affected by hunger and low access to health care are often the economically active who lack productive assets, the transient poor who are at risk of becoming poor because of periodic or transitory shocks such as droughts, floods, storms and pestilence and the core poor who have no capacity to generate income and therefore who face chronic poverty. The level of vulnerability is higher for the elderly, chronically ill, the physically challenged or disabled persons and orphans.

Development and its challenges

Despite the growing pace of urbanization a significant proportion of the population – over 80% – lives in rural areas. Two features of urban development are uneven urbanization and peri-urban development. Both reflect shortcomings of planning and formal land administration, which are made worse by lack of comprehensive understanding of how people find their way amidst the challenges of living in the periphery.

Over half of smallholder farmers cultivate less than one hectare. Employing rudimentary production technologies, many households produce barely an average of 75% of household food requirements. One of the underlying factors has been the slow shift to high yielding varieties of cereals (maize and sorghum for instance) and legumes, the country's staple food items. The low priority accorded to livestock production and to irrigation development, and also limited development of agricultural research and extension (Kulemeka 2000) as well as declining livestock farming due in part to decreasing grazing land, theft and diseases act as further challenges to economic progress.

Over half of the extremely poor people live in rural areas in the south. Paradoxically, the south, including the Blantyre-Zomba urban centres, hosts many symbols of national development: hydroelectric power plants; the largest national university and four of its constituent colleges; and with few exceptions the headquarters of various commercial banks, insurance companies, manufacturing companies and research institutions and agricultural research stations. If development was synonymous solely with clustering of such institutions, the south would indeed be the development hub of Malawi. The 2004–2005 integrated household survey revealed that households in the Central Region have the highest consumption expenditure while those in the Southern Region spend the least, but on literacy households in the Central Region recorded a lower rate (Government of Malawi 2005a).

Economic uncertainties and problems of poverty are not entirely economic or production related in origin and character. Beliefs, habits of thought and customs play an equally important role. So is the political system, and in particular, the failure of political leadership. Five decades into independence and despite possessing formal structures of modern bureaucracy, day to day affairs of the state are characterized by personalized political authority of the president. Development and the lack of it are centred on the presidency, from whence the power and resources of the state are exploited to dispense patronage and sustain political excesses. The process, which includes collusion with (un)suspecting donors, undermines the strategic function of the state in facilitating socioeconomic welfare. With or without a certain majority in parliament, Malawi's presidents can govern with the authority of an all-powerful despot or with veiled despotism and with utmost impunity, thanks to a selective approach to rule of law embraced by various arms of government.

For convenience, the whole 51 year postcolonial period of Malawi is bifurcated into five time periods in relation to the tenure of the presidents that have ruled: Hastings Kamuzu Banda (from 1963 to 1994), Bakili Muluzi (from 1994 to 2004), Bingu wa Mutharika (from 2004 to 2012), Joyce Banda (from 2012 to 2014) and Peter Mutharika (since May 2014). Ove time each president has failed to demonstrate that the government could be a neutral arbiter, whose role is to promote national interests, economic growth, efficiency and social welfare (see Sandbrook 1982). Most have also harboured and portrayed false impression that they represent the best thing ever to have happened to Malawi.

Having broken the federation of Rhodesia and Nyasaland and led Malawi to independence from British colonial rule, Dr Banda maintained with deceit the title 'messiah' throughout the thirty years he presided over a highly personalized and repressive regime, well known for extreme brutality and intolerance of alternative voices. For thirty long years, Dr Kamuzu Banda maintained legitimacy through a combination of coercion, political patronage, personal charisma and populist appeal (Englund 2000, 2006; Harrigan 2001). Access to public transport, markets, schools and hospitals was on condition of possession of his ruling political party's membership card. To date his Malawi Congress Party (MCP) has been unable to regain significant following in the southern and northern parts of the country. One factor leading to his downfall was the uncertain and harsh economic conditions during the early years of structural adjustments.

From the 1960s through the 1980s, Banda's regime emphasized estate-led growth, while smallholder producers on customary land were to a large extent neglected or exploited by the state and its agencies through half measures (Harrigan 2001). During the last decade of his rule, smallholder income terms of trade declined by 25%, while those of estate farmers rose by 44% (Ellis et al. 2003). Structural adjustments and political pressures, generally associated with the wave of multiparty democracy at the beginning of the 1990s, led to the first multi-party elections in 1994, in which Banda's Malawi Congress Party lost, bringing an end to three decades of his authoritarian and single-party rule. The United Democratic Front (UDF) emerged winner in both the presidential and parliamentary general elections, and the new government promised changes in the development strategy, emphasizing smallholder agriculture and private sector growth and reorientation of public expenditure toward social services (World Bank 2006).

Riding on a messianic accolade also, the regime went on to mess up the economy and the democratic promise. Political liberalization and associated reform processes became slow, uneven, and complicated (Ellis et al. 2003). One of the casualties was the state itself, given that since then it has been captured by rent seeking and patronage. The distribution of spoils of office takes precedence over the formal functions of the state. As a result, the ability of public officials to focus on making and implementing public policies in the interest of the public is severely limited. Efforts to prolong his stay as president beyond the constitutional limit of 10 years failed.[9] Since then elements of misrule are attributable to the perpetuation of the style of government introduced during the transition to the democratic dispensations. Another enduring trait is opportunistic privatization and of diversion of state resources as important sources of patronage, what Booth et al. (2006 cited in Dorward et al. 2008) described as the 'democratization' of corruption.[10] On a positive note government repealed the Special Crops Act, which had restricted smallholder cultivation of burley tobacco during much of Dr Banda's time. Another significant policy change was free primary schooling.

The introduction of free primary education resulted in a jump in enrolments of about 1 million pupils, the majority of whom were girls. The effect has been an increase in literacy from 63% to 76%, almost all of it a result of the rise of literacy among women. On the overall, there is challenge of retention. The 2010/2011 integrated household survey (IHS) showed an increase in the net enrolment rate (NER) in primary schools for children between 6 and 13 years of age from 80% in 2005 to 85% in 2011. However, half of all pupils drop out before reaching the fifth class of primary school and before many have attained functional literacy and numeracy. In addition, the primary school education is challenged by an acute shortage of adequately trained teachers, resulting in a pupil to qualified teacher ratio of 84 to 1 (Department for International Development 2007) or worse. The national secondary net enrolment rate (young people aged between 13 and 17 years old) is very low at 13%, with district level rates ranging from 3% to 23% (Government of Malawi 2012a). A very small percentage (only about 0.4%) of the population proceeds to university or other tertiary institutions (University of Malawi 2012). It is clear that access to education beyond primary school is very limited for reasons related to limited capacity in public higher education institutions and higher fee rates in private higher education institutions.

Information on education and literacy is significant for a number of reasons. It is essential for planning and for evaluating existing policies. Over time, it has also become quite clear that education is a major determinant of living standards. Apparent low education levels accompanied by low literacy rates and low economic growth are among the defining characteristics of a developing country (Government of Malawi 2005a). Also, it is important for poverty reduction because education empowers the poor, the weak and the voiceless by providing them with better opportunities to participate in national development. Education is therefore a fundamental building block for human, political and socioeconomic development.

With regard to the repealing of the Special Crops Act, smallholder farmers eventually responded quite positively, and there was a rapid growth in the number of smallholder farmers engaged in the growing of burley tobacco. However, accelerated structural reforms involving the reduction of price controls, the increase of prices to smallholder farmers in order to stimulate production, the restructuring and privatization of statutory corporations, and the devaluing the currency caused harm to most smallholder producers. Most smallholder farmers have been unable to take full advantage of the reforms. Enduring challenges have been shortages of arable land and high prices of fertilizer (Harrigan 2001; Stambuli 2002). Shortages of land in many areas of Malawi have resulted in short fallow systems, continuous cultivation, extension of farming to marginal land where the loss of top soil is massive and have led to the decline of soil fertility or the reduction of the soil's organic matter, especially where crop residues are also used for fuel as a result of the growing scarcity of fuelwood. With respect to problems of access to fertilizer, the government introduced the universal provision of small packs of fertilizer along with maize and legume seeds under the starter pack programme in 1998. Critics have pointed out that the emphasis on fertilizer was a response to the failure of many farmers to earn their livelihoods from farming. These rural producers continue to face various difficulties in accessing fertilizer despite interest in its use for the production of food and non-food cash crops (Dorward et al. 2008).

The period from 2004 onwards appeared initially as one of reconstruction. There was awareness of the need to create conditions that would enable the poor to contribute towards reducing their poverty. What was missed, however, is that poverty cannot be reduced unless there is development-oriented good governance, political will, security and justice. Efforts of a couple years before to reform the land situation, for instance through the formulation of the national land policy (2002) and the land resettlement scheme funded by the World Bank, were piecemeal and cosmetic. Apart from major projects involving road construction countrywide, construction of additional grain reserves, the green belt initiative which is yet to take off, the river port development project in Nsanje, the University of Science and Technology, and the scaling up of HIV/AIDS treatment, other developments before and since then have been compromised by unnecessary policy shifts as if poverty reduction and growth are mutually exclusive.[11] Except for the targeted fertilizer subsidy, which led to substantial surplus of maize output for a period of close to five years – though its sustainability is now in question – the impacts of some initiatives on rural development and livelihoods security were hard to discern. This became clear when the country suffered serious and intolerable deficits in foreign exchange and fuel supply over the 2011 – 2012 years.

Deteriorating rule of law and problems of economic governance and of human rights culminated in nationwide demonstrations in mid–2011 (with the main activities taking place in major urban centres) and the death of some of the participants at the hands of policemen and with most of the deaths happening in Mzuzu. The deaths of demonstrators at the hands of police was generally felt to be regrettable as it raised serious questions on the effectiveness and the credibility of the much acclaimed police reform program, generously bankrolled by the international development partners. The circumstances under which the deaths occurred are murky, and for political expedience no effort has since been made to establish the truth,[12] thus paving a way for a fourth messianic space. It needs noting, however, that calling the event nationwide demonstrations is a misnomer as it gives undue weight to the work of urban based non-governmental organizations (NGOs), many of which pursue narrow and foreign driven agenda.[13]

Since the end of the first quarter of 2012, immediately following the unexpected demise in office of the president, most alleged repressive laws that earned Malawi a bad reputation have been repealed. For a time multilateral lending institutions reopened credit lines, and bilateral donors resumed disbursements of grants and loans. Several daunting challenges remained to be solved, including enhancing home grown sources of foreign exchange and upscaling indigenous economic activity. The worst fears among ordinary people remained growing insecurity, skyrocketing prices of essential consumer goods, high inflation rates and price instability arising from the devaluation of the currency by over 100%, although the official devaluation rate at the time was 49%. The real value of wages was eroded significantly by over 50%. In a manner that signified a repeat of the 2001–2002 scenarios, the then ruling party presided over the depletion and disappearance of thousands of tons of grain from strategic reserves under circumstances that are by and large dubious.

For the first time, Malawi witnessed cash transactions that are nothing but sheer and orchestrated plunder by the political party in power, where pay-outs amounting to billions were made to individuals and companies with no business contracts with the government[14] and through some dubious out-of-court settlements. Initial estimates indicated on contracts only significant losses of over 20 billion Kwacha in dubious payments to over 50 private companies.[15] Big loads of cash were recovered from civil servants and businesspersons, some of which have been convicted and currently serving prison terms. Other court cases at various stages of prosecution. It became evident that the ruling party could not be exonerated from the looting of the treasury.

While the looting of public funds of this magnitude continued, for the first time in the history of Malawi, district and rural hospitals suspended for months the provision of meals to patients, ostensibly due to budget constraints.[16] Health workers bemoan gross underfunding, shortage of basic drugs, shortage of food, and numerous deaths of patients from curable conditions. Given the deteriorating state of many services, including failure of the state to pay teachers, agricultural extension workers and nurses, it became evident that piecemeal measures, whatever the content, could not translate into economic prosperity and political trust.

Perhaps, and this is another dimension to the uncertain narrative, the electorate cannot decipher good from bad, rhetoric from reality, leaders from opportunists? This is not correct if attention is paid to disapproval and condemnation of the practice by civil society groups and the unpalatable ridicule of the leadership by ordinary citizens expressed through print and online media and phone-in radio broadcasts on private radio stations. Bizarre labels not complementary in any way have been used liberally to describe the leadership, which is an indication that the public is unimpressed with the status quo. Troubling trends, many of which have been mentioned above, include escalation of poverty, socially and politically engineered tensions, inequality and a myriad of associated social consequences, such as a rise in crime, destitution, squalor, disease and avoidable deaths associated with public hospitals which have virtually become waiting shelters for food starved patients and the dying.

Concluding reflections

The foregoing analysis indicates that lack of development or to be poor is to be without the means to live a dignified life. Generally it means a lack of capability as well as possibilities to produce, acquire and command control over means of production and social reproduction. It includes inability to direct energy, time, and reason to matters that can contribute to overcoming and breaking the roots and vicious cycles of deprivation, exclusion and unequal power relations are constantly at play in the global periphery.

Lacking and sometimes denied opportunities for self-actualization many poor people take comfort in activities that provide meagre returns, sometimes taking sides in conflicts for and on behalf of political elites cum oppressors. They become blind to the fact that they are by and large denied opportunity to define and realize their own interests because of uncertain access to resources, employment and income opportunities. It is the competition for resources that has compelled many people in Africa to adopt an inward-looking ethnic consciousness. Political and religious leaders have been too

27

good at exploiting ethnic as well as regional identities, both real and imagined. Competition happens between ethnically differentiated people living in rural and urban environments, but it is often in the urban centres where intense competition is manifested with great divisive force.

Notes

---

[1] Geographically located between latitudes 9^0 45' and 17^0 16' south and between longitudes 33^0 and 36^0 east. In terms of geopolitical position Malawi is landlocked surrounded by Mozambique to the south, east and west, Zambia to the west and Tanzania to the north. Owing to the large size of the neighbouring countries, Malawi is in comparative terms a dwarf among giants.

[2] Twenty-eight percent of the land is in the North, 38% in the Centre and 34% in the South (Msilimba 2007).

[3] Lake Malawi is the third largest lake in Africa. It is about 570 km long, ranging from 16 to 80 km in width, and lying at 475 metres above sea level. On average the lake stores 90 km^2 of water (Government of Malawi 2010).

[4] Main arable and tree crops are maize, rice, tobacco, sugar, cotton, groundnuts, timber, tea, coffee, and rubber. The country's potential to produce some crops has not been fully exploited.

[5] Deforestation is linked to major land use changes happening in the tropics where equatorial rainforests are eventually declining for causes related to lumbering, settlement development, agriculture and the biodiesel industry. These activities contribute to the release of carbon dioxide from biomass and from soil organic matter.

[6] The Malawi Demographic and Healthy Survey (MDHS 2010) showed that infection rates vary with sex and age. For instance, among women aged 15-49, the HIV prevalence rate was 13%, while among men within the same age range it was 8%. However, HIV prevalence increases with age for both women and men. Among women, HIV prevalence is highest among the 35-39 age group (at about 24%), which is six times the rate (of 4%) among

women aged 15-19. For men, prevalence increases sharply from 1% among men aged 15-19 to 21% for men aged 40-44, and then it drops thereafter.

[7] Rural poverty in Malawi, www.ruralpovertyportal.org/web/guest/country/home/tags/malawi

[8] World Bank (2016) http://data.worldbank.org/country/malawi (accessed on 16 January 2016)

[9] Muluzi's time in office was for some time referred to as a lost decade. More than thrice, donor-government relations became particularly strained as a result of donor nations' claims of economic mismanagement and governance failures, and weakening of government capacity.

[10] Concern and lack of action on rising corruption forced the IMF to withhold balance of payment support; the Department for International Development (DFID), the European Union (EU) and USAID suspended development assistance, while the government of Denmark terminated development projects and withdrew from Malawi entirely.

[11] A policy shift, from a focus on poverty reduction to a focus on growth, is apparent in relation to the implementation of the Malawi Poverty Reduction Strategy (MPRS). The MPRS was in effect for a period of three years only, given that implementation came to an end in the 2004-05 fiscal year. A decline in poverty levels, from 54.1% to 52.4%, was reported over the period (Republic of Malawi 2007). Whose poverty was reduced remains a mystery. While the MPRS was in its implementation phase, the Government of Malawi developed the Malawi Economic Growth Strategy (MEGS) (July 2004) as an alternative to the MPRS. The rationale was to expand sectoral sources of growth, deepen and sustain the gains from agriculture, and make the economy less susceptible to external shocks such as changes in the terms of trade, political developments in southern Africa, unfavourable weather patterns, and fluctuations in external aid flows (Republic of Malawi 2007). A review of MPRS, *Comprehensive Review of the MPRS 2005*, informed the development of the Malawi Growth Development Strategy (MGDS) (Republic of Malawi 2007).

[12] Reports from online news sources and eye witnesses indicate that most of the victims were shot hours after the planned demonstrations, some while looting shops and businesses owned by Chinese traders.

[13] Some activists unsympathetic to practical everyday needs of the majority they claim to represent and some have on several occasions disappointed the public by lack of clarity of purpose, infighting and over exaggerated sense of influence nationwide. Some take activism as a stepping stone for political appointments to governing boards or state corporations,

presidential advisors or membership of public commissions that serve no purpose at all but to fleece the public purse.

[14] Agnes Mizere 'Malawi's Anti-Corruption Bureau Arrests a public officer, *Daily Times*, 14 October 2013.

[15] *Daily Times*, 17 October 2013

[16] MBC-TV reported on its 8.00 PM news bullet on 16 October 2013 the resumption of meals for patients at Nkhatabay District hospital after some four months. The hospital was able to resume providing meals following a donation of food items by Vizara Rubber Plantations, a private company operating in Nkhata Bay district in northern Malawi. The reporter, however, emphasized the timeliness of another donation of food items from the state president's private foundation a couple of days earlier. Banda demonstrated that desperate situations call for desperate measures. One such measure was the aborted attempt to subvert the will of the people expressed freely in tripartite elections. She attempted but failed to nullify election results that put her erstwhile political enemy in the lead. The uncertainty that followed was a matter of grave concern affecting everyday economic and social life and the future of various government projects.

Chapter Three

The Meaning and content of development

Important concepts covered in this chapter are poverty, inequality, underdevelopment and sustainable development. Lack of clarity about them may inhibit understanding of how various social, economic and political relationships actually come into being and also how they are likely to operate in the future. However if it is to be defined, development should entail liberation from external political and economic domination, meeting people's needs and realizing various potentials on terms and conditions that advance human dignity both in the present and in the future. Achieving development requires men, women and children taking their places as responsible, dignified, and productive citizens. For countries of the global periphery, challenges may include overt and sometimes covert attempts to orient the state: bring the state down either by sowing seeds of political instability or dislocating the economy to reinforce foreign cultural interests.

The meaning of development

There are diverse understandings of the meaning and requirements for development (Desai and Potter 2008; Seers 1969; Streeten 1995; Szirmai 2005; Todaro 1992). This was not so in the first two decades immediately following the end of World War II, a period stretching through the 1950s and 1960s. Then, development was but a synonym for aggregate economic growth, with an increase in real income per head and broadly of a country's gross national product (GNP). Development policies of the time placed an emphasis on growing the GNP, capital accumulation and industrialization.

Import substitution and export-oriented manufacturing opportunities were to be exploited to the full to achieve take-off and rapid economic growth.

During the late 1960s and early 1970s, awareness of socioeconomic inequalities that often accompany GNP growth influenced a rethinking of the meaning, content and direction of development to encompass both growth and qualitative change in social and economic conditions. It was recognized that growth in GNP is not a sufficient condition for overcoming poverty. What may be desirable and effectively constituting development at a particular time, place and in a particular culture may not be desirable at other times at the same place or other places and indeed within the same culture and socioeconomic milieu. Katar Singh, among other scholars, pointed out that development in the context of a particular society should perhaps comprise desirable objectives which that society seeks to achieve (Singh 1999).

The sections that follow will provide insights into a) development as a synonym for progress, b) ideology and development in developing countries, c) development and geopolitics, and, d) what should constitute development in the coming decades.

Development since the Second World War

In everyday talk within developing countries, discussions on development hinge how to grow economies and overcome poverty. The term 'poverty' has been used almost interchangeably with other concepts such as deprivation and vulnerability (Chambers 1989). In material terms, poverty refers to a state of being unable to eat and dress properly and afford proper housing. Perceived of as a process, however, poverty carries the meaning of lack of development and the making of inequality whereby development implies moving towards getting rid of conditions that define the poor or the state of being in poverty and he creation of conditions under which socio-economic equality is conceivable and achievable.

The poor are those whose socioeconomic situation is low. It implies some hidden or less overt processes at play. These involve challenges that lead to either inactivity or inadequate prospects and lack of opportunities to improve the social and economic situation at individual, household and societal levels. At the household level, poor households are those that are in a state of deprivation and lack prospects of ever improving their lot. They are unable to meet basic necessities of life such as food, clothing, shelter, primary health care and security of life and property. The basic needs approach to poverty, however, takes into account the minimum nutrition, housing, health and education requirements only without which life becomes intolerable and full of uncertainties. With regard to what may be conceived as tolerable conditions, current theory makes a distinction between 'relative' and 'absolute' poverty.[1]

Relative poverty describes an individual's or a group's level of wealth in relation to other individuals or groups. It means that some people are poorer than others, and therefore it emphasizes levels of inequality within and between societies. Relative poverty becomes recognized as a real problem when the difference between the richest and the poorest is intolerable in the sense that the poor, while not actually destitute or starving, are nevertheless deprived of many of the goods and services that others take for granted. Absolute poverty, on the other hand, represents poverty in its raw and extreme form. It means lack of food, lack of cash income and lack of assets that can be liquidated or exchanged for food, clothing and other needs. Hence, absolute poverty is a condition in which it is not possible to obtain the basic needs of life or where deprivation is so severe that the basic needs of life can scarcely be met at the minimum level required for survival and human dignity. This is a state of existence in which the overall needs are not satisfied due to lack of enough purchasing power or means for self-provision.

In the case of absolute poverty, it is possible to set a cut-off point based on income, consumption, expenditure or some other proxy below which people are considered to be absolutely poor and above which they may not be poor. The cut-off point, otherwise called the poverty datum line, delineates average expenditure on goods and services per day. It is currently fixed at US$1.90 per capita or US$693.5.25 per year. The cut of point has been adjusted twice recently from US$1.00 to US$1.25 and now to US$1.90 per day. Each time the cu-off point has been adjusted upward the effect has been to reclassify border line cases and the obvious result has been increase of numbers of those below the poverty line.

Recently, although quantitative studies that define poverty as a lack of adequate income are still widely consulted and cited, but they have been complemented by studies that define poverty in terms of lifestyles, attitudes and behaviours (Szirmai 2005). Ironically, despite pledges by governments in Africa and indeed all the less developed countries to alleviate poverty, usually in national development plan (NDP) or political party manifestos, improvement in the socioeconomic aspects of poor people appears a far off dream. Pledges by international development agencies (World Bank, International Monetary Fund (IMF), Food and Agriculture Organization (FAO), for instance) to eradicate poverty are full of rhetoric. Seventy years of international commitment to development and fifty years of independence from colonial powers, for many Africa states, few people have risen from the ranks of poverty. High population growth in poverty-ridden countries often means more poor people eking a meagre existence from pressurized resource bases and economies. Economic growth and development assistance over the decades have not been adequate for the eradication of poverty and in some cases have been part of the recipe for greater uncertainty.

Since the end of the Second World War, scholars and politicians and 'development workers' – often outside of developing countries and sometimes in consent with leaders of those countries – have promoted a succession of ideas, slogans and recipes: 'the idea that large-scale injections of capital are the key to development ('big push'); the 'small is beautiful' movement; human capital as the missing link in development; the green revolution as a technological fix for agricultural development; community development; appropriate technology; basic needs; integrated rural development; self-reliance; delinking from the world economy; the New International Economic Order; market orientation and deregulation; promotion of the informal sector; structural adjustment policies; or sustainable development' (Szirmai 2005). Concepts such as concerned participation, ownership and partnership were introduced in the development debate more recently (Olsson and Wohlgemuth 2003). The UNDP popularized the human development index, which pays attention to literacy, longevity and income. The implied normativity in the various ideas, slogans and recipes and the speed at which some have been tried and then discarded is dumbfounding.

The question to be posed is: Will there be any progress worth living and celebrating? Experiences in the developing world or the global periphery suggest that remarkable socioeconomic transformation has been achieved in some countries and much more progress will occur in the fastest growing countries, namely Brazil, China and India (UNDP 2013). For the slow growing economies of sub-Saharan Africa, it will take much more time for real and sustainable progress to take off. However, reflecting on nuce sounding slogans used in the past decades such as the development decade, sustaibanle development, new international economic order, halving poverty as in millennium development goals (MDGs) and sustainable development goals (SDGs) and make the discourse on development sound like a game in which the only established rule is that new rules shall be invented as need arises to prolong the game. Development looks like a game or play where actors keep erasing and changing the year in which 'development goals' would be reached. Meanwhile developing countries keep on vying to become HIPC (highly indebted poor country) and on their knees begging donors to be recognized as such. As one of the anonymous reviewers of the manuscript observed:

'Ha. Reminds me of a play I saw at the CCF in Bamako or Dakar (can't remember which). Actors had small chalkboards. They keep erasing and changing/advancing the year in which "development goals" would be reached. The play was very satirical, as you can imagine. And full of acronyms. And folk were vying to become HIPC (highly indebted poor country) and on their knees begging donors to be recognized as such. And the dates kept being erased on the small chalkboards. And advanced. And finally the village nut, or wise person, (or both or neither) hard to know, erased all years from his/her chalkboard, admitted that s/he would NEVER be all developed, wrote the current year on the chalkboard and decided to enjoy life… today…'

The pace of development in former colonies, however, is perpetually controlled by patronizing outside others. This is the fate of being geopolitically weak, marginally productive and highly vulnerable to long lasting economic and political machinations. It is not a secret that each decade since independence in the 1960s, or earlier and also later, former colonial masters, other powerful states mainly from the west, and some powerful multilateral institutions and sometimes proxy domestic institutions have in one way or another operated in both overt and covert ways to undermine national sovereignty, territorial integrity, and legitimacy of governments. They have proceeded to subjugate and contain economic aspirations in many African states, including Malawi, and their peoples. Himmelstrand warned of the dangers of succumbing to this colonial pattern of pseudo-development noting that colonial rule interrupted endogenous development and monopolized indigenous entrepreneurship and mercantile capabilities in line with its interests. A pattern of unequal exchange solidified and became entrenched thanks to luring colonial international trade founded on the satisfaction of overseas market interests. These processes continue to discourage the search for self-grown development initiatives and smother the search for greater political and economic autonomy (Himmelstrand 1994). The nude lesson is that economic independence, or even healthy interdependence, cannot be declared, legislated and decreed like political independence.

Colonialism and its present manifestation of neo-colonialism are markers of the exploitation of the dependent nation by the master nation. True independence from colonial rule would entail definite structural changes, for example use of resources including land, minerals, and manpower to produce food and generate wealth with which to feed people even in situations of rapid population growth. However, this structural change has not taken place, which accounts for food insufficiency, livelihood insecurity, poor health and dwindling or low living conditions, and high levels of malnutrition and child mortality alluded to already. A complementary structural change is ensuring farmers' access to basic tools needed in food production. In countries with serious arable land deficits, including nations reticent to upset colonial indiscretion in land ownership, tools could be provided for other productive activities through which income could be generated to purchase imported food. These are just two examples of many structural changes that have not taken place.

No wonder that most developing countries lack control over the direction and pace of their development. For capital, they have to look outside to borrow or beg, sadly enough, even for small projects. Providers of capital proceed to prescribe how it should be used, sometimes confusing and fusing ideology for development.

Ideology and development

The developing world's uncertain development is not due to a dearth of ideologies. On the political front, one of the most revolutionary legacies of the Second World War is decolonization of Africa and Asia, which commenced with India attaining self-rule in 1947. Ghana led the way for British Africa exactly a decade later. The most notable significance of this turn of events is that the rallying call that inspired popular mobilization throughout Africa was a commitment to development. Most first generation post-independence African leaders were in principle developmentalists. Many, like Kamuzu Banda of Malawi, emphasized the virtues of hard work, individual striving and self-reliance. One of Banda's notable statements in this regard was: 'To me '*Wanangwa*' [freedom] must not mean starvation. If you are hungry you are a slave. Freedom must mean free from hunger, poverty and nakedness.'[2] Lack of food and clothes are internationally recognized as rude manifestations of poverty. That poverty and want persist, despite the purportedly best – yet somehow scandalous – efforts of foreign governments and institutions acting with the tacit approval of African governments, should serve as a reminder of the unfinished development business of the past six decades.

The United Nations charter, among other areas of concern and commitment, sets out to work towards the socioeconomic progress of all peoples. Many UN agencies, including the United Nations Development Programme (UNDP), United Nations Children Education Fund (UNICEF), and World Food Programme (WFP), claim to be working towards the alleviation of global poverty and suffering, in particular, in the developing world. Other multilateral agencies claim to complement the work of the UN and national governments. These include the World Bank, the International Development Association (IDA), International Monetary Fund (IMF) and various international non-governmental organizations (NGOs), like World Vision and OXFAM. With this wide ranging group of interested parties, persistent under development is either a manifestation of the enormity of the challenge or the insufficiency of effort. At another level, it is the utmost betrayal of the hopes of those who are poor.

Political economist and late president of Malawi Bingu wa Mutharika (2004 – 2012), wrote in the opening chapter of his book, *One Africa, One Destiny*: 'At the time of independence, many political leaders in Africa had a great dream that they would control their economies and their destinies' (Mutharika 1995: 1). He and many other African leaders instead found themselves in a difficult position of negotiating Africa's uncertain development. New forms of colonial domination (neo-colonialism) operate to keep former colonies tied to former colonial masters and to other powerful states and international organizations that operate as if they were established for that purpose. Multinational and transnational corporations (MNCs/TNCs), international trade agreements like the General Agreement on Trade and Tariffs (GATT), the World Trade Organization (WTO) created to regulate trade and tariffs worldwide, and, more recently, the International Criminal Court (ICC) serve mostly the economic and political agendas of rich nations. Even a not so careful look into the global economy shows that powerful MNCs are principal agents of underdevelopment.[3] Although MNCs have offices and/or factories in different countries, usually they have a centralized head office where key decisions are made and global operations coordinated. Nearly all major multinationals are American, Japanese or Western European, such as Nike, Coca-Cola, Wal-Mart, AOL, Orange, Toshiba, Toyota, Honda and BMW, and have, along with other institutions already mentioned, perfected mechanisms that entrench the subordination of poor countries to socioeconomic considerations, political requirements and progress of rich nations.

Not all MNCs/TNCs are alike, but the dominant position they occupy in everyday life is a threat to many national interests, not just economic ones. An economy dominated by multinational corporations is nothing but an economy managed from foreign cities. An economy in this situation is not any better than a colonized economy. On the one hand, multinational corporations create jobs and wealth and provide technology in countries in need of new technological development. On the other hand, they operate wherever doing so suits the profit motive, including in countries with low to despicable human rights records and environmental standards.

41

MNCs exploit poor countries for their natural resources, including cheap, unregulated and non-unionised labour. They may even raise part of their capital within host countries but export all profits. To maximize profits, they may limit workers' wages while also enjoying a host of state-sponsored protectionism. They may even contribute to erosion of traditional cultures and challenge national sovereignty with impunity. Many have budgets that exceed by far those of many small countries. For this reason they play undue political influence in economic and political affairs in host countries. Also worrying is the impact MNCs have on indigenous enterprises. They reduce competition and free enterprise since stiff competition created by the entry of giant MNCs in peripheral markets endangers local manufacturers. Of late there has been growing interest and recognition of the adverse effects of MNCs even in western countries.

At another level, technological dependence is part of the process and system of exploitation of neo-colonial economies by metropolitan economies. Industrialized countries are reluctant to transfer latest technologies. They may instead sell 'yesterday's' technologies, which might be 'dirty' and no longer allowed in industrialized countries because of health, safety and environmental considerations (Wilson 1990). They are more interested in the exportation of raw materials cheaply from developing countries and the importation of finished products at exorbitant prices into developing countries. Therefore, development at the global periphery is at the mercy of the geopolitical and resource considerations of rich nations and MNCs, whether these are stated in explicit or implicit terms.

Development and global politics

Intoxication with wealth, power and influence lure presidents and prime ministers and even civil servants and civil society activists from some rich countries into the belief that they are predestined to govern other nations. As Mugabe once put it, 'Countries such as the U.S. and Britain have taken it upon themselves to decide for us in the developing world, even to interfere in our domestic affairs and to bring about what they call regime change.'[4] African leaders have learned diversion tactics. For Malawi, failure and falling popularity at home has often been compensated by international endorsements, including honorary doctorates awarded in recognition of reported achievements that hardly tally with achievements on the ground. Visits by foreign heads of state or heads of international organizations, actual intentions notwithstanding, have also been exploited as demonstration of approval of leadership style. The irony is obvious, paternalism is entrenched.

Britain maintains close ties with her former colonies and dominions throughout the Commonwealth is another device. As years turn into decades, and decades into a century, it can only be hoped that many people in peripheral commonwealth countries will begin to question the need for the neo-colonial organization. This is likely to happen where British covert, rather than the declared, interests are threatened as the case of Zimbabwe has shown. Robert Mugabe has chosen to be controversial rather than bow to pressure to compensate white farmers for land that was initially stolen from the native population. Mugabe manifested a rare boldness when he declared: 'If the choice were made, one for us to lose our sovereignty and become a member of the Commonwealth or remain with our sovereignty and lose the membership of the Commonwealth, I would say let the Commonwealth go.'[5] Recently, Gambia followed suit, pointing at the neo-colonial instincts of the predominantly white member states of the Commonwealth. Aside the wanton disrespect for liberal democratic values by these regimes, these instances highlights the paradox of the international political economy and the mismatch in power relations that imply that few dare question the West.

Colonialism was a multifaceted cultural process.[6] Given the likelihood of many an African leader towing, if not chained to old colonial ties, colonialism will remain a potent force guiding and misguiding national development ambitions. Have Africans become unimaginative followers of foreign control, ideologies, fashion, merchandise and recently cultural ways? The unmistakable and enduring future challenge is that an economy dominated by powers elsewhere, regardless of whether that control is economic or political or cultural or military, is not any better than a colonized economy. As Katar Singh put it a nation is not independent if its economic resources are controlled by another nation just as political independence is meaningless if a nation does not control the means by which its citizens can earn their living (Singh 1999:25).

Development as a normative concept

Over four decades ago Dudley Seers wrote that development is inevitably a normative concept and almost a synonym for reductions in poverty, unemployment, and inequality (Seers 1969). In the view of the South Commission (1990:10), however, development should be construed as a process that enables human beings to realise their potential, build self-confidence, and lead lives of dignity and fulfilment. As the South Commission further noted, development ought to be a process which frees people: 'Development has therefore to be an effort of, by, and for the people.' The South Commission recognised development as a situated phenomenon, situated in the context of social, economic and political organisation, with the consequence that citizens owe obligations to society, which in essence implies that development means growth of the individual and of the community of which the individual is a part (The South Commission 1990: 11).

Development ought to include the pursuit of social justice and the equitable distribution of resources and opportunities and of development efforts and outcomes. Deprivation of any form is out of order. Deprivation would mean or lead to lack of necessities and the means to survive economically, politically and, sadly so, culturally. The deprived would become unable to feed and clothe themselves and would have no access to services others take for granted, and in the case of deprivation of food and water, be on the brink of death. However, even for deprived people, development should mean provision of and access to services in health, education, transport, potable water, off-farm employment opportunities, and renegotiation of existing structures and relationships that counteract progress. More generally, drawing on Watts, development should always involve men, women and children taking their places as responsible, dignified, and productive members of their communities (Watts 1969). Development therefore is not mere building up of one skill or one aspect of life. It includes challenging economic, political, and social norms, values and customary practices that lead to exclusion be it on the basis of social, biological, religious, political and more broadly cultural grounds. A privileged position for men in any society is not fair. It cannot be justified. For both economic and social reasons, the costs of ignoring gender inclusion and equality are many, including inefficient allocation of resources for farming (agriculture) and consumption, divided societies and poorer life for all.

Currently, there is a strong tide towards mainstreaming gender in development planning, implementation of development programmes and projects, and in their monitoring and evaluation. Gender, as a theoretical and practical reality, is a development concern in its own right. Gender relationships forged by men and women on the basis of their social position are increasingly questioned, and equality should be recognized as an integral component if development is to be anything meaningful.[7]

In mainstreaming gender, there is little disagreement on certain aspects defined as priorities by women and men and policymakers alike, and often the absence of disagreement relates very much to the fact that the realization of such needs has often worked well for the preservation and reinforcement of gender division of labour. Strategic needs, however, revolve around dismantling structural barriers to meaningful participation. Strategic needs include issues women identify because of occupying positions subordinate to men, and they relate very much to challenging divisions of labour, the exercise of power and control of institutions as well as infringements in the areas of legal rights, domestic violence, equal wages, access to education, access to credit, and rights to land and property. Given the social rigidities sanctioned by customs and traditions, law and religion, strategic needs are quite often difficult to achieve. Financial resources and the ability to mobilize, organize, and lobby are important requirements. However, resource poor women may lack agency to reflect on strategic needs because of the urgency of meeting immediate and practical requirements.[8]

Paths to development

The foregoing discussion shows clearly that there is no single path towards development. Barnett (1988), in *Sociology and Development,* described three broad paths: development from within, development as interaction between societies, and development as interpenetration.

Development takes place from within when changes, both major and minor, arise as the result of inventions and critical reflection on thoughts, beliefs, and economic, political and social systems. This sort of change could be referred to as autonomous development. Development may also take place via interactions between societies, countries and regions of the world. Changes may occur because of interactions with outside others, for example, other countries such as the industrialized and capitalist west or multinational enterprises, both of which are also paradoxically blamed for under developing and exploiting poor nations. Foreign investment and greater involvement of MNCs are part and parcel of this sort of change. The Green Revolution in India was supported financially and technically by the United States Agency for International (USAID) (Singh 1999). Major infrastructure and technological development in many Africa countries is also financed in large part by outside partners, including China increasingly. Development can also occur as a consequence of interpenetration, whereby changes result from any number of complex interrelationships within and between societies. It is easy to distinguish these different pathways for the purposes of analysis, but in reality they overlap and intermingle in complex ways.

From the 1980s, discourse on economic liberalization and sustainable development opened useful perspectives on development. Following growing awareness of challenges posed by enormous damage to the environment, specifically the depletion of natural resources, the mantra in the 1990s was sustainable livelihoods, sustainable poverty reduction and sustainable development. Sustainable resource use remains a key feature in livelihoods approach, poverty reduction efforts and development as highlighted in the Brundtland Report (1987) and echoed in the Earth Summit report (1992) held at Rio de Janeiro; popularly known as the Agenda 21. The Brundtland Commission report titled *Our Common Future* emphasizes that development ought to guarantee satisfaction of needs and aspirations of the present generation without compromising the capacity of future generations (World

Commission on Environment and Development 1987). Harrison (1996), however, noted that by combining development (inevitably a value laden concept) with sustainability (which is non-operational and reformist) the development community has arrived at the doubly vague concept of sustainable development.

There are a number of questions which have not been addressed even by the advocates of sustainable development goals (SDGs). Is sustainability a process of development and/or an outcome of development? Central to this question are issues of time, scale, intergenerational balance and locus of emphasis (Luke 1995: 21-22).

'First, sustainable for how long: a generation, one century, a millennium, ten millennia? Second, sustainable at what level of society: individual households, local villages, major cities, entire nations, global economies? Third, sustainable for whom: all humans alive now, all humans that will ever live, all beings that will ever live? Fourth, sustainable under what conditions: for transnational contemporary capitalism, for low impact Neolithic hunters and gatherers, for some future space-faring adventurers? Finally, sustainable development of what: personal income, social complexity, gross national product, GNP frugality, individual consumption, ecological biodiversity?'

Despite growing awareness of the problems of applicability, the concept of sustainable development has gained supremacy in development thinking. The central tenet is that development, if taken to mean satisfying needs and wants in the present, should not be detrimental to meeting

49

needs and wants of future generations. This futuristic orientation is also problematic (Desai and Potter 2008). It can be hard for the poor to operationalize sustainable development; it is tempting for them to disregard the future to provide for the pressing needs of the present. In Malawi, the rich and those in leadership positions fall into the same trap. It appears, as Anne Ferguson writes on gendered and agricultural development, that programs have adopted the term 'sustainable' and continued with business as usual (Ferguson 1994).

Achieving sustainability requires regulation and robust planning to prevent wastage of resources. Development can occur without planning (autonomous development) but it is likely impossible to guarantee some socially desirable level of living for all. However, in many developing countries integration of economic and political decisions is a recipe for corruption.

Although there is a lack of legal consensus on the definition of corruption, it is generally understood as the abuse of public office for private gain. The World Bank (1997:8) as cited in Akçay (2006:33) suggests that:

> Public office is abused for private gain when an official accepts, solicits, or extorts a bribe. It is also abused when private agents actively offer bribes to circumvent public policies and processes for competitive advantage and profit. Public office can also be abused for private benefit even if no bribery occurs, through patronage and nepotism, the theft of state assets, or the diversion of state revenues.

In most cases, proceeds or illicit assets obtained through bribery, patronage or theft are transferred from one jurisdiction to another in order to disguise the source. Eventually it becomes difficult to distinguish licit from illicit funds and assets. Estimates suggest that cross-border flows of proceeds of corruption, criminal activities, and tax evasion amount to between US$1 trillion and US$1.6 trillion per year. In Africa an estimated amount in excess of US$148 billion or about 25% of GDP is lost in this way.[9] In public procurement alone, corruption diverts 10 to 20% (sometimes as much as 50%) of contract values, while bribes received by public officials in developing countries and countries in transition amount to between US$20 billion and US$40 billion per year or an equivalent of between 20% and 40% of official development assistance (ODA).[10] These loses are enormous when perceived from the development point of view. They are a lost opportunity to invest in the development of agriculture, health, education and infrastructure.

Notes

[1] Poverty became an important issue in the nineteenth century, and systematic attempts were made to define, measure and understand it. Among the earliest studies were qualitative accounts that described the lives of the poor, for example, Henry Mayhew's report on *London Labour and London Poor* (1851) (Social Policy for Development, Source: www.sagepub.com/upm-data/9518_010378ch02.pdf). Quantitative studies of poverty based on census data emerged around the same time, but they were subsequently superseded by household surveys based on direct interviews aimed at obtaining more detailed information about incomes, expenditures, housing conditions and family size. The early studies laid the

foundations for current ones that measure poverty levels based on such indicators as gross domestic income and purchasing power parity, and in relation to the human development index and the poverty index, among others.

[2] From a speech made by late president of Malawi Dr Kamuzu Banda at a mass rally marking the end of the 1985 annual gathering in Mzuzu of the then ruling party, the Malawi Congress Party. Part of the speech was reported in the news article titled: 'The Ngwazi spells out meaning of Wanangwa', *Malawi News,* October 12-18, 1985.

[3] By definition a multinational corporation (MNC) is a corporation that is registered in more than one country or that has operations in more than one country. On the role of multinationals in the globalizing world, the CEO of Coca-Cola, Muhtar Kent, had this to say: 'You can probably say capitalism is the worst model – except for all the others. ... I think we have to evolve it to make sure it is better socially connected to the people's wishes and needs and to create a better harmony in the world. ... I think it's going to end up where we have that 'golden triangle' working better with government, business and civil society. I think it can (be done). Look at our case. We can continue to grow, to invest and hire. We are a company that does business on a local basis in 206 countries. We are the most international' (Coca-Cola CEO: Capitalism needs to evolve, 5 February, 2013. CNN Business, www.cnn.com)

[4] www.brainyquote.com/quotes/authors/r/robert_mugabe.html

[5] www.brainyquote.com/quotes/authors/r/robert_mugabe.html

[6] Colonialism laid the ground for the ready acceptance and adoption of foreign cultural and ideological positions and products. Business institutions and corporations spawned in the West have operations worldwide which allow that goods designed in one country can be manufactured in another and shipped to many more, yet the profits are centrally administered in the parent country. The geopolitical ambitions of western nations have impact on all, allies and enemies.

[7] Approaches to gender have varied from eliminating barriers that limit entry into the labour market, known as the women in development (WID) approach, to dismantling patriarchy the gender and development (GAD) approach and now the UN Women. Both approaches (WID & GAD) recognize the critical need for equity in development processes. However, WID focuses primarily on initiatives targeted specifically at women such as access to credit and employment, the creation of women's ministries and so on, whereas GAD focuses on the system of gender relations in which

women are historically subordinate and attempts to address women not as a special group but as fully integrated members of society.

[8] It has been shown that practical gender interests are determined inductively as a direct reaction to needs, problems and interests that are immediate and based on social conventions such as gender specific division of labour and roles allocated to women and men. Strategic gender interests are developed deductively from analysis of suppression of women enshrined in gender hierarchies (Braig 2000).

[9] The World Bank and United Nations Office on Drugs and Crime, *Fact Sheet on Stolen Asset Recovery* http://www.unodc.org/pdf/Star_FactSheet.pdf

[10] The World Bank and United Nations Office on Drugs and Crime, *Fact Sheet on Stolen Asset Recovery* http://www.unodc.org/pdf/Star_FactSheet.pdf

Chapter Four

Space, place and urban economic informality

Development takes place in time and across space, and one such space is the urban public space. Urban public space may include public parks, pavements, produce markets, roads and streets, and vacant land. As experiences of urban vending in Malawi show, all these spaces are exposed to appropriation by urban informal economy workers, most of whom may be poor. For street vendors, use of public space invite and signify uncertain relations, both civic and symbolic. This chapter locates the dilemma associated with such use of urban public space as one of the uncertain situations that affect urban livelihoods and development.

Space, place and informality

Among geographers space was initially conceptualized as an objective physical surface or place with specific fixed characteristics upon which social and economic activities could occur and be mapped out. Social identities were taken for granted as fixed and mutually exclusive (Johnstone et al 1994). With hindsight, space is now understood to play an active role in the constitution and reproduction of social and economic relations and identities (Dear 1997). Hence, space should no longer be treated as 'the dead, the fixed, the undialectical, the immobile; it is to be understood as intrinsically operative in the construction of social power and knowledge' (Balshaw and Kennedy 2000:2).

Space is filled with politics and ideology. Natter and Jones (1997) argued that the distinction between public and private spaces demonstrates the ability of governing groups to naturalize spatial categories according to vested interests, including capitalist property relations. Through the same processes, urban space is often hierarchical, zoned, segregated and gated to encode both freedoms and restrictions of mobility and of access. Urban zoning is thus an exclusionary instrument; a subtle though effective method of segregation often on the basis of income (Balshaw and Kennedy 2000:11). Consequently, regulatory urban practices including formalization of space are in essence a condensation of social relationships through which elite power dominates even though the local urban authorities and planners might claim to be readable, neutral and transparent arbiters (Dear 1997).

Stories involving repression include that of street traders in Jakarta (Indonesia) since the 1970s on allegations of 'eating' space meant for the general public (Murry 1991). Bromley explored the repression of the street vendors in Latin American cities such as Puebla (Mexico), Quito (Ecuador), and Cartagena (Colombia) for reasons of being unfair competitors or saboteurs of established commercial interests. Other classic studies include that by Bayart (1997) and Cross (1998) in Tehran (Iran) and Mexico City (Mexico) respectively. In apartheid and post-apartheid South Africa, space politics has been a subject of continuing interest. During apartheid most informal consumers of urban spaces were street vendors, most of whom were black and for that reason suffered heavily under the apartheid policy of blacks as 'temporary sojourners' and the ideology of cities as the abode of the white population (Rogerson and Beavon 1985:234). In post-apartheid the methods deployed and rationale has shifted. In other African countries, Lesotho and Uganda, for instance, street vendors endure suppression. The *Mopheme/The Survivor* of Maseru and *The New Vision* of Kampala have carried stories of harassment and persecution of street vendors in Lesotho since 2000 and Uganda since 2002, respectively. Even in Dar-es-Salaam, street vendors are often engaged in constant struggles with the city council in what Tripp termed 'the battle over grounds' (Tripp, 1997: 158-9).

This chapter is neither on the characteristics nor the significance of the informal economy but state-vendor relations with respect to the use of public space, both in the physical and metaphorical senses. Relations take place in a context characterized by informality, where no officially recognized ownership by the user of particular urban space exists and in the case of street spaces such use contravenes the purpose assigned to the space by the formal societal system (Laguerre 1994). In some cases, such use of urban space has been seen as a reflection of declining and stagnating economies in the face of continuous rural-urban migrations and globalisation, and so it has been seen as a symptom of urban crisis in the global periphery. According to the United Nations Centre for Human Settlements (1996), urban crisis has three major components: a decline in levels of formal employment and a corresponding rapid increase in 'informal sector' activities in many key areas of the urban economy; a deterioration in both the quality and distribution of basic services; and a decline in the quality of the urban environment, both built and natural. All these changes adversely affect the quality of urban life for everyone but particularly for low income groups. In some cases, the decline in conditions of living can be squarely blamed on state failure. The state, as a

57

political and legal entity, involves complex interactions between enacted legislation and officials responsible for the day to day enforcement of legislation.

It is also the intention of this chapter to demonstrate how street vendors' use of central urban spaces has been perceived, experienced and mediated, both implicitly and explicitly by the state as well as portrayed over a period of time. The understanding here is that the state encompasses more than the executive arm of government. In fact in the view of Sandbrook (1982), the state comprises the executive, bureaucratic, legislative, judicial, coercive, and publicly controlled educational, media, trade-union and party apparatuses designed to protect national security, foster the conditions for capital accumulation, and maintain social control. The state in this instance would therefore include local city councils, the executive or national government, and the ruling party agents. The state represents the formal or front while the vendors represent the ordinary, informal and periphery. These terms are used with cognizance of post-structural theorization of the 'self' and 'other'. As Natter and Jones (1997: 151) wrote, to speak of the 'formal' or 'informal', 'front' or 'back' or 'core' and 'periphery' is already to acknowledge the constitutive power of both

The informal economy

The informal economy in scholarly circles emerged as a scholarly analysis of space of survivalists comprising initially very poor people engaged in low level income-generating activities, including the self-employed who produce goods for sale, purchase goods for resale, or offered various categories of services and all kinds of micro- to small-scale enterprises. Its intellectual history is often linked to one particular study of Frafras, one of the northern Ghanaian ethnic groups living in Accra as observed in the 1960s by Keith Hart (Hart 1973). They were noted for the variety of economic activities in which they were involved in and through which they earned a living and so changed their own income and expenditure patterns in a manner that could not be accounted for using economic tools applicable to capitalist economies. Since the late 1980s the informal economy has been associated with activities that have emerged due to the failure of developing countries to formally make the kind of economic progress that would have allowed for, among other benefits, low urban unemployment rates, reductions in national poverty rates, wages and salaries that keep pace with inflation, the ready availability of basic goods and services, functioning infrastructure, and efficient bureaucracies. In this regard, informality is more than an outcome of lack of meaningful employment, rather, as a recent write up by Keith Hart (2006) suggests, the informal economy is provoked by the failure of orthodox economic models to address a large part of the world for which they offer prescriptions.

The effects of informality, once thought to be palliative, are often seen as a threat to formal businesses (Hart 2006). It comprises activities that operate largely outside national and local legislative or regulatory frameworks. Informal economy workers have been known to subvert the order and even comfort of the urban environment by carrying out activities without regard to public health, safety and convenience, and planning or zoning regulations and practices. As a result, the informal economy is sometimes seen as inconsistent with modernity. It is swept into a pile labelled chaotic, untidy, unhealthy and illegal (Post 1996). Very few analysts, however, have blamed urban planning and politics for being heavily biased in favour of 'modern' business ventures such as banks, factory scale industrial production and high order retail and wholesale outlets (see Rogerson and Beavon 1985 for an earlier exception).

Context and approach

In Malawi, the informal economy is tolerated but not liked. Two of Malawi's presidents have claimed links to economic informality, with one in a joking manner claimed to be a cabinet minister responsible for street vendors and yet another having gained a reputation of having risen from the ranks of 'marketeers.' Laws restrict the establishment of informal businesses, new markets or vending outside existing markets. Vendors are not welcome in private spaces. Outside major banks are signposts proscribing vending within banking premises. Occasionally, vendors have been asked to vacate street stalls or risk confiscation of their merchandise.

The site of the study on which this chapter is based on is Blantyre City, Malawi's oldest urban centre. Blantyre was officially declared a township in 1895, while Lilongwe, Malawi's capital since 1975 was then a small trading village. The 1895 map of the British Central Africa Protectorate shows Blantyre as Malawi's major settlement (Douglas 2000). Lilongwe and Mzuzu are conspicuously missing. As Douglas also put it Zomba, Malawi's colonial and post-colonial capital up to 1975, was subordinate as indicated by the cartographer's lettering. Lilongwe achieved the status of a town in 1947 and Mzuzu in 1966; despite the fact that Mzuzu's place as the regional centre for the northern region of Malawi was established in 1953, when the colonial government made Mzuzu the Provincial Headquarters for the Northern Province (Jimu 2008a).

All these urban centres – Blantyre, Lilongwe, Mzuzu and Zomba – are now cities. All embody both public and private spaces. Informality thrives in public and private spaces. Street vendors, who have been the focus of studies of informality, occupy pavements and other open spaces, resulting in parallel patterns of use. By operating in areas that are not designated for vending such as carparks, bus stations, lee ways, and verandas of shop and office buildings, street vendors expose themselves to rains, winds, intense heat from sunshine, and sometimes the wrath of other businesspeople, the general public and the state. Urban space is appropriated and transformed through what Laguerre (1994) termed informalisation of formal spaces. Informalisation is often considered inappropriate, given the expectation that commercial and industrial centres embody cosmopolitanism and modernity; both of which are challenged by the practice.

The analysis relies on experiences of selected street vendors, interviews with officials at the Blantyre City Council, and public statements of leaders as reported in the print media. As the sources of data suggest, this chapter will also explore popular views about public space on which ordinary people (street vendors in focus) draw daily and the ways they situate themselves in relation to the formal view often represented in master plans, layout plans, zones, bylaws and public statements of civic and political leaders.

State – street vendors relations 1960s to 2000s

The timeframe of the field study stretched over a decade, with much of the work taking place between from 2002 to 2007. During most of this period, street vendors occupied all the busy streets in Blantyre and Limbe central business districts (CBDs). In Limbe, Market Street and James Street, from Livingstone Avenue to Limbe Produce Market, were then pedestrian bazaars. Blantyre city authorities came to accept pedestrianization of these parts of the city (Blantyre City Assembly 2000). The same pattern was reflected in Lilongwe where Malangalanga, Devils Street and many other streets were all turned into pedestrian bazaars. To a limited extent, Mzuzu and Zomba also manifested some level of pedestrianization.

Then, as is it now, street vendors provided a wide range of goods, including newspapers, cosmetics, jewellery, watches, wallets, ladies' handbags, second-hand clothes, electronic and radio devises, and foodstuffs. For much of the period, going back to the late 1960s, relations between the street vendors and city authorities were not cordial. Bylaws enacted in 1966 and amended several times later forbid street vending, except where a license has been issued. The bylaws give the Blantyre City authorities mandate to regulate vending by limiting the number of valid licenses at a particular time, presumably to minimize crowding in the streets. The initial fee for a vending licence was set at £1 per month or £12 per year. In the first five months, only 30 people bought the licenses[1] and in subsequent years vending has been going on without the vendors applying for licenses to do so. In the 1970s, penalties for contravention of the bylaws were a fine of £10 or imprisonment for two months for the first offence and a fine of £50 or imprisonment for six months for the second and subsequent offences. In case of continuing breach, the penalty was fixed at £1 every day during which the offence continued.[2] The penalties were revised to K100 and three months of imprisonment for the first offence and K200 and imprisonment for six months for the second and subsequent offences. Further contraventions attracted a fee of K2.00 per day during the period the offence continued.[3] But the state largely failed or was reluctant to enforce the bylaws.

Public attitudes towards street vendors have been mixed, even associating street vending with crime as in the following opinion in the 1960s: 'There is one practice which must be dropped [...] some young men who sell fruits and vegetables along Victoria Avenue [...] These people can be, and are very disturbing, someone parking his car to do serious business is only hindered by one of these unscrupulous and irritating men.'[4] Sentiments of this nature have to different extents been used to legitimize state repression and persecution of street vending. Persecution of street vendors in Blantyre and other cities was particularly pronounced during the one-party dictatorship, that is, from independence in the mid-1960s to the early 1990s. It is noteworthy that street vending has attracted significant attention of three of the five presidents, namely Hastings Kamuzu Banda (1963 – 1994), Bakili Muluzi (1994 – 2004) and Bingu wa Mutharika (2004 - 2012). As early as 1976, President for Life Dr Banda urged city authorities to keep the city clean as follows: 'We believe in cleanliness, grace and elegance.' In 1988, some 12 years later, his words were stronger: 'Cities were meant for civilized persons, and in that regard people should be able to differentiate life in the city from that of the village by the way you look after the city. If you should be proud of the city don't bring village life into the city' (Jimu 2003, 2005). During the same period, a mayor of Blantyre City described vending in the following words: 'We are disturbed by these people who are trying to spoil and detract us in our efforts to keep the city clean. The city has therefore decided to take drastic measures against all illegal vendors.'[5]

During the 1970s through the 1990s, many street vendors were beaten and their merchandise confiscated without compensation. In 1990, about 80 street vendors in Blantyre were arrested, charged and fined about US$6.00 each at the prevailing exchange rates at the time or instead allowed to serve one month in public works for, in violation of the Blantyre City bylaws, hawking without licenses.[6] Following the transition to multiparty rule, in November 1995, 30 street vendors in Limbe sought legal aid for compensation of property worth K35, 954.00 destroyed by police and city rangers. Although section 28 (2) of Malawi's constitution adopted in 1994, following the transition to multiparty democracy states that no person shall be arbitrarily deprived of property, the city council refused to pay compensation arguing that the city rangers and the police officers involved in the process were enforcing the law. The understanding being that the street vendors 'do not have legal business premises.'[7] Arrests, confiscation of merchandise and court appearances of street vendors have been few and isolated. In many instances the matter of street vending has been settled 'amicably' between the apprehended street vendor and his or her captor.[8] Gifts of money or other things cement relations. In case of new or incorruptible officers, the street vendors either alert each other by whistling to escape, what may also be called 'passive networking' or some form of instantaneous and hushed communication established among atomized individuals with common interests by virtue of a visibility facilitated through common space (Bayart 1997). In some instances street vendors put up a fight. For instance, in 1992 the Blantyre City Council decided to step up its campaign against street vending to 'treat this disease now.' The campaign proved fruitless and costly. The street vendors fought back with stones, sometimes breaking windscreens of vehicles used by city rangers, and in one such incident, one of the city council security men lost two fingers in a struggle with street vendors.[9] Other strategies used by the street vendors to elude confiscation of merchandise include hiding merchandise in bushes by the roadside, only taking a few with them at a time. The failure of the city council to keep grass along streets short often worked to the benefit of the street vendors. Some street vendors hid goods in dustbins whenever city rangers approached.[10] Other street vendors chose to carry merchandise in travelling bags, and they disguise themselves as ordinary pedestrians or travellers. These strategies represent passive, nevertheless creative, ways of fighting marginalization. They show that individual street vendors as social agents are quite capable of devising ways and means of seeking 'redemption from victimhood' (Nyamnjoh 2000:34) amidst uncertainties of various kinds and magnitude.

In the mid-1990s, following the change from one party rule to multiparty rule, street vendors anticipated immediate changed in policy and tactics from repression and tolerance to formalization. The reality, however, was that, although the transition from one-party authoritarian rule to multiparty and liberal democracy introduced remarkable changes in the areas of human rights and freedoms (Englund 2002), these changes did not concern street vending. Street vending in the mid-1990s and the beginning of the century was characterized by confrontation, with periods of relative calm, between street vendors seeking to assert rights to trade and city authorities seeking to enforce zoning and 'orderly' use of street spaces. The political leadership was unsure of how to deal with the growing agitation for recognition among street vendors. In the midst of uncertainty, the population of vendors continued to grow. Blantyre and Limbe had in 2006 a population of over 6000 street vendors. At one time in 2002, street vendor associations in Blantyre and Limbe had registered a total of 4697 vendors, of which 1700 operated in Blantyre and 2997 in Limbe. These vendors used vending spaces informally allocated by the chairpersons of their associations. The chairperson exercised chiefly powers with respect to the allocation of vending spaces, which included arbitration of disputes over space (Jimu 2003). All the registered street vendors claimed at the time that their chairman allocated them the space on which they were vending. New entrants had to come through the chairperson, and they were required to pay some money as a token of appreciation. This scenario signalled bipolar authority over street spaces, one formal and legal, the other informal but not necessarily 'illegal.' Nevertheless, the street vendors organized their activities in pragmatic and utilitarian ways that did not conform to any legal and planning standards, thus legitimizing what is otherwise illegitimate.

Relocation of street vendors has been pursued with less vigour. Operation *dongosolo*, as the state nicknamed its drive to rid streets of informal vending in 2006, was welcomed with applause in the print media. Little was said about the origins of street vending and the fact that street vending had been a characteristic feature of urban life in Malawi and that of Blantyre City way back to the 1960s.[11] The economic citizenship of the street vendors was disputed as if what vending stood for was completely out of touch with the reality of the majority. For instance, one of the issues should have been the fact that street vending thrives because it administers to the needs of the public. That informal vending represented a grassroots response to problems of rising unemployment and growing urban poverty and is in fact one of the opportunities created by economic liberalizations in the 1990s.[12] Taking these issues into account would have demystified street vending. Although the local city council and the state police succeeded in freeing the streets of street vending for some time, they did not crush the capacity of ordinary street vendors to think, imagine, influence or change urban order. This will be explored in the subsequent sections.

Location rationality and economic rights

For street vendors, the best location for lucrative business is any place with high levels of pedestrian and vehicular traffic (Jimu 2003). Because the busiest streets are considered the best location, forcing the vendors to relocate to less conspicuous streets or sites off the streets would deprive them of direct access to actual and potential clients. Given a choice, they would chose to operate along major streets where the probability of trading is relatively high. They dread any threats to relocate them from the streets filled with regular clients and spontaneous buyers. Clients include people going to or knocking off from work. Street corners and road junctions appear to be prime sites. Relocation, whether negotiated or forced, is perceived as an assault on vendors' livelihoods, even their bodies and souls. Resistance to relocation should be perceived in this light. Enoch, who had lived in Blantyre for over 17 years at the time of fieldwork in 2002, was involved in the selling of second-hand shoes in Limbe. He claimed that when most of the vendors in the main streets were relocated in and around December 2001, he lost touch with most of his regular clients. Although his business picked up later on, he likened relocation to changing wives, which he noted as having the same effect of breeding poverty. Forcing street vendors to operate in flea markets is often resented because such markets are not ideal for very small businesses. In the streets, the situation is considered open and free: trading is fast, and the playing field is level for both old and new players. It could therefore be argued that streets as public spaces represent spaces of economic opportunity.

Streets as fluid spaces of opportunity

As early as the 1960s, Hart (1973) saw in the informal economy a buffer against instability and insecurity of work and income among the urban poor. Street vending, as a sub-sector of the informal economy is thus a survival strategy for individuals, families and groups of people relegated to work and eke out meagre existence in 'the dungeons of the informal sector' (Rogerson and Hart 1989:29). It also represents an avenue of legitimation and recognition for people who find the 'promises of modernity are fast becoming a broken dream for all but an elite few' (Nyamnjoh 2002:118, 120). In the case of Blantyre, street vending is a means to earning income and meeting necessities of life such as food, shelter and clothing. Most of the street vendors identify poverty, limited employment opportunities or lack of gainful employment as the factors that drove them into vending. Most are also constrained by low levels of education attainment and lack of employable skills required in the formal sector (Jimu 2003). Most operate barely at subsistence level. Peter, one of the street vendors engaged in selling medicines in Limbe, summarized his situation in the following words:

> 'What else can I do apart from street vending? I dropped out of school in primary school. I can't find a suitable job. I am married with two children. I take care of five nephews and nieces, children of my deceased sister. Should I become a thief?'

Desperation of this nature is a recurrent feature in press reports on street vending across Africa. One of the most challenging experiences is that of street traders reported for Johannesburg who were interviewed during the World Summit on Sustainable Development (WSSD) held in 2002. When their government prohibited street vending in areas frequented by participants at the Summit, the street traders organized a demonstration against what they termed 'brutality' of the police. As one of the demonstrators pointed out, 'What is sustainable development when our own government denies us the only means of survival? This conference is a sham and it will only perpetuate the existing imbalances in our society as only the rich are going to benefit from it.'[13] Similar sentiments were expressed during the 2000 eviction of street traders from the streets of Maseru, Lesotho's capital. Some street vendors complained that they, unlike the Chinese, were disadvantaged. One irate woman street vendor commented: 'We are not comfortable in our own country. Only the Chinese will survive in this country while its poor citizens will always go hungry.'[14] The feeling among street traders that as bona fide citizens of their respective countries they have a right to trade in the streets underscores how street vending represents a spatially diffused opportunity to legitimate economic ends. Any effort by local authorities to evict the vendors is therefore rightly felt to be a contravention of a fundamental right to livelihood and economic development.

Besides suggesting that street vending is an economic opportunity, Peter's sentiments cited above also highlight the morality of street vending in contrast to anti-social behaviours such as theft, prostitution and destitution apparently associated with urban crisis in the global periphery. Most of the street vendors consider themselves as legitimate and responsible members of the 'public' who have the right to access and use various public spaces. For example, street vendors often ask: What is wrong with using public space to make ends meet while at the same time administering to the needs of the public – by providing goods and services on terms that are negotiable? Beyond that, street vending has the potential to stimulate small-scale and micro production and encourage the development of local entrepreneurship and a market for small formal manufacturing firms. By all these accounts, street vending does not pose a threat; rather it complements state efforts towards poverty alleviation, widening access to goods and services and the development of entrepreneurial culture. Yet, it is the contribution to poverty alleviation that has received much attention, at least as the following section illuminates.

Street vending and poverty alleviation discourse

Poverty alleviation has been embraced as a development fad in many African countries, following the promulgation of poverty alleviation strategy papers sponsored by the international donor community in the 1990s. In the run-up to the first ever multiparty general elections in 1994, political parties promised heaven on earth – which undoubtedly included the freedom to engage in economic activity. Very often, street vendors refer to promises made then and suggest that street vending could be part of poverty alleviation strategy in Malawi. Being part of the government's poverty alleviation policy, until the beginning of 2006, street vendors saw themselves as complementing the poverty alleviation agenda of the government. On one occasion, some street vendors called on the then state president to come out in the open regarding his perception of street vending. One of the points of reference was freedom to do business: 'Let him deny if he never promised us freedom to conduct our business in town. He told us that even in South Africa street vending is legal. Now is this the freedom he meant when we were being chased [...]?'[15] In essence, this call was a call to freedom to pursue individual or group goals within a broad social and political frame of reference that emphasized conviviality between collective interests and individual creativity and self-fulfilment. Harassment, persecution and relocation prevent street vendors from contributing to poverty alleviation. Thus understood during consultation meetings leading to development of the Vision 2020 Project in Malawi, one of the street vendors charged that the vision is an empty promise in the making, noting that:

> 'Promises have been made before and we know this vision is also another promise. As vendors we want immediate practical solutions, not future scenarios, to our problems. Do you start building a roof to your house before the foundation?'[16]

By implication, needs and not scenarios should be yardsticks when defining use of public spaces, irrespective of conformity or lack thereof to some standards. Standards are not bad but where standards are based on or promote prejudice they cease to function as they should. It appears that this has been the trend as relations between street vendors and the state have evolved over time.

Attitudes and prejudices against street vending

The appropriation of spaces for street vending is often associated with numerous problems some of which are: erection of stalls that block the streets, inconveniencing the free flow of pedestrian and vehicular traffic and excess littering, which stretch the capacity of city authorities to keep cities clean (Jimu 2003). Also, food vending poses health risks, particularly the threat of food-borne diseases (Rogerson and Beavon 1985; Rogerson and Hart 1989; Jimu 2003). Another fact is that street vending encourages crowding of people in the streets providing havens for criminal elements and anti-social activities. These concerns show that street vending violates aesthetic, social and economic values appropriate for cities (Bromley 1998). It also implies that 'modernity' is inconsistent with the presence of vendors in the town centres (Cross 1998). Yet at this moment in time when poverty alleviation and economic empowerment are major concerns, should modernization be articulated at the expense of the livelihoods of the poor? This is quite often the challenge to urban planning in the developing world. First world cities provide planning models, making urban planning and politics heavily biased in favour of big business ventures and against the myriad of unregulated activities (Rogerson and Beavon 1985). Suffused with the ideology of modernization urban planners consider street vendors an obstacle in the way of modernization.

In the case of Malawi, local city authorities and the national leaders have since independence emphasized the need to keep the cities distinct. Reference could be made to calls by the first head of state as early as 1976 urging the city authorities in Blantyre to keep the city clean. Mary Battiata described Dr Banda's Malawi as 'Its cities are free from squalor'.[17] Certainly this was in contrast to cities in neighbouring countries as well as the situation in the rural areas. A point to be emphasized is that during the 1970s and 1980s any presence of street vendors could have been perceived as a negative feature of a regime not keen to be associated with disorderly conduct. The rhetoric of cities as distinct from the rural areas was echoed by Dr Banda's successor who was apparently supportive of street vending: 'how do we distinguish kuNtaja from Blantyre'.[18] Civil servants, whose income status is not very much different from that of the average street vendor, are often used as instruments to advance standards that they themselves cannot uphold. For example, city rangers who survive on street foods are required to police the streets. They do feast on food that they confiscate, which is otherwise condemned as unhygienic. Similarly, the problem of littering and waste disposal is erroneously associated solely with street vending when street kids, pedestrians and motorists have been part of the problem. It is probably true, as one commentator remarked that the worst littering agents are probably the super markets.[19]

Reorganizing vending

Despite that the street vendors have been repeatedly forced to relocate off the streets they continue to exert pressure on the state by occasional comebacks. The Ministry of Local Government and the city assemblies are constantly challenged on how best to accommodate the informal vending by among other measures funding construction of flea markets. As of 2002 the goal was to construct six flea markets: two markets each in Blantyre and Lilongwe, and one each in Mzuzu and Zomba. The intention was and it still remains to contain and prevent street vending. Three markets were completed and occupied by the vendors in Blantyre, Lilongwe and Zomba by 2008. A fourth and fifth market in Limbe and Mzuzu are now completed and almost ready for occupation.[20] As the experience in Blantyre, Lilongwe and Zomba demonstrated between 2002 and 2006, the street vendors were initially against occupying the flea markets. Some vendors were particularly angered by the prospect of having to start paying market fees. Some argued that their businesses were too small and would be unprofitable to be grounded in an enclosed marketplace. Yet, others demanded that the government should provide them loans before they could relocate off the streets, presumably to re-capitalize or expand businesses. Actually, others were seeking some form of compensation in respect of being relocated. None of these conditions were satisfied when the vendors were relocated in 2006.

Although freedom and flexibility of street vending leads to 'eye sore' scenes, street vendors appear to be indispensable political allies, particularly during general elections. The vendors constitute an electoral group whose significance cannot be dismissed, especially in Malawi's multiparty political system. By virtue of their numbers and the ease with which they can be mobilized for particular political cause, the vendors can make or break political aspirations (Cross 1998 on Mexico). Experiences in the past decade have demonstrated that street vendors can also be a costly liability. Basic examples are the reluctance and failure of the street vendors in Limbe and Blantyre to repay a loan amounting to K10 million and the initial reluctance of the vendors to occupy flea markets in Blantyre, Lilongwe and Zomba between 2002 and 2006 after the government had already spent over K40 million for each structure (Jimu 2003).

Closing reflections

Towns and cities have been centres of economic and social development (Jimu 2008a). New ideas and new and exciting jobs and socioeconomic opportunities continue to be linked to urban centres. Past and present decisions about land use, transportation and economic development; political processes and representation; and social planning contribute remarkably to the structure of urbanization. The economic challenges that recent rural-urban migrants encounter, at least in the initial stages of their stay in towns and cities, revolve around limited employment opportunities and slim chances of ever getting meaningful and rewarding employment. By implication, many accept any work that comes their way. Those with low education attainment are more vulnerable (Jimu 2003), and as has been observed already, most of them end up in the informal economy. Informality, though difficult to define, is characterized by unconventional actions well aimed at meeting needs by ordinary people.

One of the arenas that manifest that the state could be a curse to popular aspirations of ordinary citizen is the way in which public space is imagined and concretized. This is evident in the negativity and persistent persecution of street vending by the state, the 'dictators' and 'democrats' alike. The concept 'state' has been used loosely as constituting an amalgam of both the national and the local governments, although in reality it is also a personification of the leaders as individuals or agents of the state. Actions of the state have been contrasted with those of the street vendors representing formal-informal or core-peripheral dichotomies. Those who carry out so called informal activities within the spaces of the streets are thus exposed to all forms of state sponsored restraints. While city authorities and the national government represent and advance formal interests and are capable of enforcing those interests by persuasion, intimidation, and sometimes force, street vendors seek to appropriate and to creatively use public space as a place of self-employment. Lack of common understanding on what constitutes appropriate use of urban spaces is always a source of tension and sometimes of confrontation, what was characterized as the struggle for the city by Rogerson and Beavon (1985) writing for South Africa and the battle over space by Tripp (1997) writing on Tanzania. In the context of Blantyre and other urban centres in Malawi street vendors locate their activities as responses to economic hardships, and they perceive the state and city authorities' quest to keep the city clean, 'safe', 'orderly' and 'attractive' as pretexts to marginalize anyone who is peripheral to the political and business establishment in the literal and metaphorical senses. It is important to appreciate the 'survival logic and the spatial-economic behaviour' (Post 1996:158) of the vendors as one form of negotiating allocation and misallocation of public goods. On the survival logic, it suffices to state that for many informal economy workers a stay in the towns and cities is predicated on opportunities in the informal economy. The alternatives to such a life are various forms of antisocial occupations, including theft, prostitution and destitution. Life outside the towns and cities would require engagement in some form of poorly resourced agriculture, a subject to be considered in the next chapter. The spatial-economic behaviour of street vendors could enrich the understanding of policy makers and planners of complex issues involved in the use and governance of public space. Urban planners might benefit from being transparent arbiters and urban planning and zoning might thus cease to be alien and disgraceful exclusionary instruments.

Notes

[1] 'Hawkers are warned' *The Times* 4 May 1967.

[2] *The Times* 4 August 1974 . Malawi used the British Pound up to 1971, when the Kwacha was adopted as a local currency.

[3] Local Government (Urban Areas) (Blantyre City Council) (Markets) By-laws, 1972.

[4] 'Now the street beggars have been cleared from the streets' *The Times* 5 January 1967.

[5] 'Council warns street vendors' 4 May 1989.

[6] 'Over 80 street peddlers fined' *Daily Times* 9 July 1990.

[7] Chinyeke Tembo wrote in *The Nation*, 30 November 1995- 'Vendors to sue mayor' by Chinyeko Tembo

[8] *Daily Times*, Wednesday 26 January, 1994 'No end to street vending problem'

[9] Two quotations from the same newspaper story titles: 'War against street vending hots up: Mayor closes shop', Daily *Times* 7 February 1992.

[10] 'One time at a bus depot a street vendor hid a packet of yellow buns in the dust bin when he saw the city council rangers' *Malawi News* 12-21 May 1993 by Pilirani Kachinziri.

[11] 'Campaign to keep city clean' *Malawi News* 27 June 1967.

[12] President Bakili Muluzi is quoted (in a state of the nation address in the national assembly) as saying 'I am proud to say that those who are doing

small-scale business as vendors or hawkers are prospering in our liberalized economy' (*The Nation*, 3 June 2002- 'Vendors Please Muluzi')

[13] *Mmegi* (Gaborone) 30 August to 5 September 2002

[14] *Mopheme/ The Survivor*, 'No Bread on Plates as Children go Hungry', 5 September 2000.

[15] 'CHEATED - vendors cry for their freedom'- *Daily Times* 15 July 1994.

[16] 'Vendors vision way out of sight' *The Nation* 13 August 1996. At a consultative meeting attended by street vendors and market vendors.

[17] The Herald Tribune (US) of 13 August 1988, quoted in *Southern African Annual Review 1987/88*, vol. 1: country reviews. Centre for African Studies, University of Liverpool 1990.

[18] President Bakili Muluzi speech inaugurating the MALSWITCH centre on November 2002. Indirectly blamed the street vendors for contributing to uncleanness in the Blantyre.

[19] 'Vendors: an opportunity, a menace' *The Nation,* 12 April 2002.

[20] Temporary shelters were in the interim erected in the flight path in Mzuzu city at a cost of K6 million while expensive ground works were going on a few metres away at the site of the new flea market.

Chapter Five

Agriculture and the development impasse

While food is the main product of agriculture, agriculture is also a major source of income and a means towards expanding rural employment opportunities, generating foreign exchange earnings through agro-exports and as a source of raw materials required for agro-processing industries. The dark side of the debate in many developing countries agriculture has not grown fast enough to realise its potential as a source of food and capital. It has with few exceptions not performed well as an engine of economic growth and poverty reduction. This chapter attempts to discuss facets of this predicament. Given the subsistence orientation, many smallholder producers do not have much to sell, their income levels tend to be low and precarious, and these severely affect their capacity to access and adopt innovations. It is hard to imagine a situation whereby smallholder households could be free from vicious cycle of poverty or graduate to a virtuous cycle of prosperity without price incentives, with or without better farmer organization and appropriate technology.

Development as agricultural related crisis

Agriculture includes both crop and animal production but most discussions tend to focus disproportionately on food and cash crop production. In economies dominated by the agricultural sector the lack of development is an agricultural related crisis that includes food insecurity. Yet, food crisis is not an entirely agricultural problem since it is not just a result of lagging and insufficient agricultural production but often part of a larger crisis of economic management and the development impasse in the global periphery.

As argued since Berry (1984) quite often agrarian crisis is to be associated with chronic balance of payment deficits, rising foreign indebtedness, inflation and deteriorating standards of life. Smallholder farmers who happen to be the backbone do not have their own economy and therefore a lagging and non-prosperous smallholder production does not constitute a crisis of a separate mode of production. Although smallholder farmers may appear to be peripheral to capitalism or in a state of transition between purely subsistence and commercial orientations, development of capitalism in agriculture may not lead to immediate demise of smallholder farming.

Rural poverty explained in relation to the performance of the agricultural sector is manifested by a multiple of factors not only local but also international. Among the many factors to be considered for analysis are unequal access to land, technical advice and credit required to facilitate acquisition of farm inputs, undeveloped transport systems, markets and unreliable prices and the phenomenon of exhausted land (Nayaran 1997). To understand the role that agriculture can play in rural and national development process it is pertinent also to examine and understand each of these factors in order to appreciate how they contribute to rural impoverishment. Such approach has demonstrated that rural poverty or lack of rural development is never a self-inflicted phenomenon. Rural and agricultural populations are not always poor because individuals, families and ultimately communities enjoy luxury of idleness, engage in unwise expenditure or lack intelligence.

Rather, to appreciate the situation there is need to understand the development of capitalism and the commoditization of agriculture and consequently the effects they have on long term livelihood security. Inadvertently lack of rural development and high levels of rural poverty arise from processes which concentrate power and resources at different spatial scales from the international to the local and vice versa (table 5.1).

Table 5.1: Creation of rural inequality and rural poverty

Level	Processes	Effects
International	1. Colonial exploitation 2. Postcolonial unique exchange 3. Developed world investment and repatriation of profits	Division between rich and poor countries
National	1. Unequal exchange between rural and urban sectors 2. Cheap urban food and low farm prices 3. Main investments go to the urban industrial sector.	Political and economic power is concentrated in the hands of urban middle class
Rural	Local elites, large landowners, money lenders, merchants and bureaucrats possess the power and most of the established and new resources.	Polarization of rural society. Impoverishment of smallholder farmers and households, especially female-headed households

Source: Adapted and modified from Dixon (1990: 55).

Most of the poor in Africa live in rural areas and depend on agriculture for their survival. This dependence is both direct and indirect. It is direct in situations where they live by growing food and cash crops and raising livestock. It is however indirect where they live by working on other peoples' farms or by trading agricultural inputs and output. Therefore, agricultural stagnation implies low returns for different groups depending on farming for survival and in many cases contribute to poverty levels. Growth of agricultural production and agricultural incomes could benefit the rural poor and it could potentially lead to poverty reduction, though it may help the non-poor more than the poor (Cleaver and Donova (1994) at least as trends since colonial times seem to indicate.

To begin with, during the colonial era settlers exploited African labour not by transforming Africans into proletarians but by mobilizing pre-capitalist modes of production to yield surplus to settler farmers instead of transforming them into capitalist economies. For many decades into the post-colonial period smallholder farmers have been prohibited directly or indirectly from producing cash crops of their choice. Where they have been free to grow some cash crops they have had to sell to monopolistic state enterprises and intermediate buyers sometimes before harvest and at depressed prices or let surplus production to waste because of lack of local markets or appropriate technologies for its preservation and transportation to distant markets. Various policy interventions have failed to address needs of smallholder farmers on terms that are socially just.

Prejudices inherited from the colonial time imply that smallholder farmers have to continue working constantly hard in order to survive. Part and parcel to colonial project the colonial government imposed several taxes like hut, head or poll taxes, which in the absence of or constrained opportunities to produce cash crops forced migrant labour practices. The extraction of labour was systematically helped by land alienation under conditions that local chiefs never understood well. Eventually smallholder farmers were confined to reserves located in less fertile and drought prone areas or became tenants on land they had hitherto owned. Even access to roads, extension and credit was restricted to areas of settler cultivation. The effects of colonial political economy included disruption of the basis of pre-colonial agricultural economy- that is, the kinship units upon which domestic or lineage modes of production depend. As Berry (1984) observed the consequences of capitalist penetration for African agriculture are also reflected in the extent to which the lineage mode of production survived the colonial era and what this implies for the economic performance and position of farmers and rural communities in the postcolonial era.

The chance to create a more positive policy environment for smallholder agricultural growth at the beginning of the postcolonial period was in many countries squandered. To date in sub-Saharan Africa smallholder farmers receive producer prices set lower than world price equivalent. In many African countries governments continue to retain significant influence on the procurement and the distribution of critical agricultural inputs such as fertilizer, seeds and micro-credit. Government projects subsidizing interest rates for agricultural credit have resulted in transfer of resources to large farmers with very little corresponding credit opportunities available to small farmers.

Agrarian situation in Malawi

The scenario for Malawi is quite mixed up. Historical sources have shown that pre-colonial societies in Malawi and Africa were largely self-sufficient in food and most non-food requirements (Mitchell 1968). Based on fieldwork in the 1940s among the Yao people Mitchell observed that the population was capable of self-supporting almost entirely from its own agricultural production. As other sources have shown farming was not introduced through diffusion of foreign ideas and skills but by local ingenuity and innovation (Birmingham 1983). In what has been described as the first descriptive work of the Shire Highlands, Buchanan (1885) described life and culture in the Shire Highlands dedicating two chapters to the Chiefs and tribes and their working powers and native agriculture, industries, customs and beliefs. He talked about shifting cultivation involving sweet potatoes, cassava, ground nuts and tobacco and also of native industries involving mainly mat making and basket making. In the fifth chapter Buchanan wrote:

> 'It has been said it is of no use an English agriculturalist going to the Shire highlands to teach the natives agriculture. This, in a certain sense, is true, in another sense it is not true. They grow their own crops very well in their own way; but then their way would not suit an English agriculturalist, not be adopted by an intelligent colonist' (Buchanan 1885: 116-7). .....
> 'The crop which the natives on the Shire highlands grow chiefly is *Chimanga-* Indian corn. It is grown extensively, and thrives luxuriantly. In the Blantyre neighbourhood you may see

hundreds of acres of maize, 6 to 9 feet high, with beautiful dark green leaves, each stalk bearing on an average two ears containing three to four hundred grains each. In the month of January you take a walk out through the more thickly populated places, and you see garden upon garden of splendid Chimanga, an infallible proof that the country is good' (Buchanan 1885: 118).

Earliest recorded livelihood crisis of significant proportion had occurred between 1861 and 1863. These occurrences were linked to escalation of tribal warfare and slave-raiding and drought between September 1861 and February 1862 and between September 1862 and May 1863. These events prevented cultivation throughout southern Malawi, the Shire Highlands and the Lower Shire in particular. Then followed the famous Nyasaland famine in 1949; understood today as a human induced catastrophe in the same way as the post-independence food crises of 1981, 1991/2, 2001/2, 2002/2003, 2012/13 catastrophes. In fact retrogression set in soon before the introduction of colonial rule, but intensified towards its end. Demographic patterns presented in the second chapter, unfavourable policy shifts, and technical and environmental constraints have compounded the crisis over the years.

Throughout the colonial period rural livelihoods suffered due to deliberate policies instituted to squeeze the native into impoverishment. Natives were required to sell labour at depressed wages on white-owned enterprises. In many cases, the colonial government placed greater attention on expansion of cash crop production in order to meet the requirements of overseas consumers rather than local dietary requirements (Hull 1980). Therefore, smallholder farmers spent more time and energy on satisfying needs outside their own locale, country and continent. Instead of the settler economy providing much of the exported commodities in some case especially in the 1920s and 1930s, native production anchored the production of export goods. Much of cotton production in the 1920s in Malawi, at some point rising up to 60%, was grown by natives (Buell 1965). While it was appreciated that natives preferred to cultivate their own lands,[1] many settlers objected to cotton cultivation by the native on the pretext that it effectively interfered with labour supply on white settler farms. The contradiction to be noted is that on one hand the colonial government encouraged cotton cultivation by the native while also regulating production ostensibly to prevent price fluctuation and the acquisition of wealth by natives. One of the measures instituted was the requirement on native farmers' right from 1923 to sell cotton to British Cotton Growers Association at superficially guaranteed but depressed prices. The unfortunate situation included the condition requiring appropriation of half of profits from exports appropriated to the colonial state thereby setting the precedence for post-colonial appropriation of surplus. The resilience of the native producer meant that such measures did not discourage or even curtail native production. In fact between 1923 and 1925 native cotton production rose from as low as 797 tons to as high as 2,835 tons (Buell 1965). Going back to the period prior to the economic crisis of the 1920s, economic grievances, including illegal and oppressive conditions led to resistance movements to colonial rule across

Africa. In Tanganyika now mainland Tanzania, for example, the Maji Maji rebellion of 1905 was in part a protest against compulsory planting of cotton and the use of former Arab slavers as plantation overseers (Hull 1980). The Chilembwe Uprising in Malawi led by John Chilembwe, founder of the Providence Industrial Mission (PIM), was linked to discontent with the political and economic situations. According to the Commission of Inquiry established after the colonial government had succeeded in suppressing the Chilembwe Uprising:

> 'Chilembwe worked upon a certain degree of discontent existing among a number of natives who were tenants on the Bruce land, or had been employed there, and also among natives living on a disputed area on the border of the estate, instilling into their minds the idea that they were being injured by European planters and more especially by the A.L. Bruce Estates' (Buell 1965: 247-8).

Another form of injury was that native farmers were prohibited from growing flu-cured tobacco, which was essentially a special crop for white settler farmers only. The reason was not that natives were inefficient producers or could not cope with production requirements, but the continuation of the trend referred to above, one of giving unfair advantage to settler farmers.[2] In addition, although agricultural extension was introduced during the colonial era to facilitate the development of settler agriculture there was hardly any extension service to support native farmers.[3]

At the time of independence in 1964 the economy of Malawi was by all standards rural based. The estate sector (comprising of large foreign-owned farms) specialized in producing crops for export; while the smallholders (indigenous-owned farms) sector was oriented towards subsistence crops with a significantly small marketed food surplus of export crops. The smallholder sector acted also as the labour reserve for the plantations and for migrant labour to South Africa, Zambia and Zimbabwe (Stambuli 2002). During the following decades up to the late 1980s there was strong emphasis on self-sufficiency in food production. Dr Kamuzu Banda pursued complex mix of anti-poor and pro-poor policy elements, some of which were inherited from the colonial times. Take the example of integrated rural development (IRDP) model (Chirwa et al. 2006), the formation of the Agriculture Development and Marketing Corporation (ADMARC) to manage the buying of smallholder produce or supply of inputs like seed and fertilizer and the provision of extension services countrywide.[4] However, the effectiveness of these measures, the agricultural extension system in particular, has not been effective. Malawi Government's own *Statement of Development Policies* for the period 1987 – 96 reported that:

'It is accepted that Malawi's smallholder extension and training are not generally influencing significant increases in farmer productivity. The causes include inability to offer farmers the knowledge and support packages appropriate to their circumstances; the limited experience, technical knowledge and motivation of many extension workers; and problems in providing adequate logistical support to these extension workers' (Malawi Office of President 1987:29 as reported in (Nambote 1998)

It needs appreciating, however, that evaluation of effectiveness of agricultural extension is tedious and not an easy task because of methodological problems arising from interactions of the extension service with other supportive services such as credit and marketing, and the variability of farmers in terms of resource endowments and variability of climatic regimes. The other challenge is that quite often agricultural extension service is perceived as well as portrayed as low priority area. There is an assumption that extension activities are of questionable benefits to productivity and rural development (Nambote 1998). To date agricultural extension seems to have very little impact on the majority of smallholder producers. Among the many reasons include lack of appropriate technologies, high rural illiteracy rates; and confusion between extension service and input supply, in particular with the supply of fertilizer. Lack of enough trained staff, problems of financing, in adequate transport, inadequate supervision and monitoring, poor incentives for field staff and poor governance of extension clubs are to date some of the enduring challenges.

These challenges were analysed further by the Malawi Economic Justice Network (MEJN) in its review of performance of various government departments in the early 2000s. MEJN reported serious shortage of extension workers noting that many farmers in Malawi do not have access to advice from extension workers, although 68.3% of the farmers interviewed lived in areas covered by an extension worker. The survey highlighted serious shortfalls in the number of extension workers.

About 52% of the extension workers interviewed complained of high numbers of target farmers. Then about 1,500 extension workers covered 3,000 agricultural extension sections; with the extension worker/farmer ration of 1:1800-2000 farm families against an ideal ratio of 1:750 farm families.[5]

In March 2005, the Department of Agricultural Extension Services reported that it had 2,880 established positions. In October 2004, the vacancy rate of the extension workers was at 68%. Yet the government had stopped training extension workers in the 1990s due to lack of funding and ill-informed perception that the country had excess personnel. The problem was later worsened by a high annual turnover of staff estimated at 20%, mainly due to deaths, resignations for greener pastures, and retirement (Ministry of Agriculture 2005). To date, the extension service is underfunded. Some extension workers lack of adequate training and as such they do not meet training needs of farmers, including training in areas identified recently as critical to agricultural transformation such as agri-business, irrigation development and livestock production. The paradox is that government and development partners are encouraging smallholder farmers to begin taking farming as a business, to adopt winter cropping instead of relying solely on rain fed farming, and to diversify into livestock production.

Another important measure since the late 1990s is the introduction of safety net programmes for resource poor smallholder farmers aimed at increasing production of food. The safety net programmes employed in this connection include targeted input programme (TIP) involving free packs of inputs to resource poor farmers implemented from 1998/99 to 1999/2000 seasons; the Agricultural Productivity Improvement Programme (APIP) sponsored by the European Union providing inputs on credit to resource poor farmers in 1998; and the Farm Inputs Subsidy Programme (FISP) funded by the government of Malawi, the Department for International Development (DFID) and other international agencies (Chirwa et al. 2006; Kadzandira 2007). In the 2001/02 season the number of beneficiaries of APIP went down from 160,000 to 41,800 due to high default rate in the previous year. TIP also popularly known as the starter pack, involved provision of one free pack of fertilizer and seed to poor households provided solely to promote household food security. The programme was unsuccessful at targeting the poorest people in many rural communities (Lawson et al. 2001). This challenge had much to do with the difficulty in correctly identifying the poorest families, unwillingness of local communities to single out poorest families, and the feeling that differentiation among the poor is culturally unacceptable.[6]

Nepotism weighed in more in the review of the 2001/2002 targeted input program (TIP) by MEJN which reported that 70% of the respondents had received the 'starter packs'. Of the recipients 52.4% applauded the programme for improving yields. At least 56% indicated that they achieved an increase in maize yield of 216 kg per hectare compared to the previous years. The increase was from 1,046 kg/ha in the 2001/2002 to 1,262 kg/ha in 2002/03 growing seasons. About 47.6% of the respondents indicated that the TIP initiative failed to achieve the intended outcome. Factors contributing to failure were rather different compared to those outlined in the review report by Lawson et al. (2001). Bad weather (drought or floods), late delivery of inputs and incomplete packs featured prominently. For those who benefited, 62% of the respondents felt that the targeted population deserved to receive the packs while 38% reported injustice in the manner the initiative was mismanaged by the chiefs and politicians. The general feeling among those discontented was that the packs were unfairly given to friends and relatives of the chiefs, and there was too much political interference, unfair distribution skewed against people considered to be sympathizers of opposition political parties.

With respect to the 2005/06 farming year, when input subsidy programme was reintroduced, farmers were issued with vouchers to enable them buy two bags of subsidized fertilizer. Initially, smallholder farmers with vouchers had 70% subsidy on fertilizer prices. Later the amount of the subsidy went up when the price was slashed to K500 per bag weighing 50kg. In a study by Kadzandira 2007) chiefs and other stakeholders who were distributing the coupons had not discovered that each voucher was an equivalent of cash. When this was discovered in the 2006/07 season, chiefs took advantage of the structures put in place to oversee the allocation. Many vouchers were sold rather than distributed as planned. Some vendors were reported selling fake coupons. In some cases smallholder farmers were cheated by those working for the state controlled outlets for subsidized fertilizer such as ADMARC markets and Smallholder Fertilizer Revolving Fund of Malawi (SFFRFM) shops. Staff of these outlets were not giving back changes amounting to K50 to clients who paid K1,

000 for one bag of fertilizer at the official price of K950 or K100 to those who paid K2000 for two bags of fertilizer officially going at K1900. Some vendors who had good relations with the selling points staff made business out of the sales by offering to buy fertiliser faster but at a fee ranging from K50 to K500 (Kadzandira 2007). Every year, non-beneficiaries blame local leaders and village development committee members for exclusion. Also, late delivery of fertilizer and seed, favouritism and corruption were reported.

Looking into the future

It is clear that poor planning, ill-conceived policies and programmes and inefficient implementation could stifle smallholder production much more than the lack of needed programmes. For the sake of progress, policy makers and planners need to reflect on the extent to which land, labour, input, credit and price policies are developed and implemented from the point of view of fostering smallholder production. In setting targets there is a need to inquire whether measures put in place could indeed stimulate small farmer production. Considering the primacy of research and technology in development, there is also great need to reflect on the degree to which allocation of funds for research is structured in relation to needs and aspirations of smallholder producers as well as the large scale producers. Subsequent sections reflect on some of the dimensions isolated above.

Prices, markets and smallholder producers

Prices levels of agriculture output could encourage and discourage innovation hence the pertinence of the argument for better prices with or without price liberalization policy. The simultaneous liberalization of prices of outputs and inputs has been observed to erode benefits of price increase for farm out of smallholder producers. As Cromwell noted in the 1990s the liberalization of the agricultural sector in Malawi led to a decline in the real value of producer price increases through increased input costs. Private traders did not move into crop marketing as much as expected in part due to lack of credit and suitable infrastructure. The effect of those that entered the market was generally to increase inter-seasonal variations in market prices (Cromwell 1996). These experiences raise several pertinent concerns relating to effectiveness of market liberalization. Among them, the extent to which the private sector is willing and its capacity to fill the gap left by departing state enterprises? Another question has been a concern over insufficient competition which could imply replacing state monopoly with private monopoly. Both concerns have implications on smallholder farmers' responsiveness to price incentives.

One of the core questions in agrarian debates has been the extent to which smallholder producers respond to price incentives. In other words, are the smallholder producers amenable to the process of commoditization, and what is the linkage between rural household producers with capitalist production? Goren Hyden argued some decades earlier that smallholder farmers tend to be conservative, resistant to change and less willing to expand production because they cherish what he termed economy of affection. Writing almost at the same time Williams added that small-scale producers are not only bound by tradition but also suspicious of individual betterment which often leads to a lack of imagination and also to resistance to innovation (Williams 1982). The gist of this contention is that smallholder farmers regard agriculture as a way of life (tradition bound production) as production is oriented towards survival needs. Change may not be valued for the sake of it. The contrary position has been smallholder producers are rational. That is, they respond to income and other incentives by among other measures expanding production. This is manifested in a number of ways. For instance, labour input and size of land devoted to particular crops. Evidence indicates that small-scale producers devote more land to crops which give the highest return in terms of income. This view has been echoed by Cromwell who observed considerable inter-annual variation in the proportion of land allocated to each crop, primarily in response to changing producer and input prices. So Cromwell argued that smallholder farmers are price responsive (Cromwell 1996). Cromwell was right. For some time the adoption of cash crops like tobacco, coffee, tea and cocoa, soya beans, paprika, sunflower by small-scale producers is part of the evidence that smallholder farmers are capable of responding to and exploiting existing market opportunities.

Quite earlier Jones (1960) argued on the rationality of rural producers in Africa that they are 'economic men'. His contention was rural producers are 'capitalist' whose decisions are based on utilitarian calculation of relative costs and returns to allocation of scarce resources to alternative ends. This calculating rationality could be substantiated using observations about Ghanaian cocoa farmers, where among other points of interest some of them have always regarded cocoa growing as a business. They acquired land according to commercial criteria, mobilize savings and credit, reinvest part of their profits in the acquisition of new land, financed public facilities such as roads and they have always taken long-term view in deciding on investments (Williams 1982).

Despite recent changes, for example liberalization of prices of agricultural output, governments tends to control the marketing of agricultural products directly and indirectly by setting terms and conditions under which smallholder trade may take place. The mandate and sometimes monopoly rights exercised by marketing boards stand out as a point of reference. Historically the objective of marketing boards was to stabilize producer prices, to reduce inter seasonal price variations and stabilize foreign exchange earnings (Lyimo 1999). However, the marketing boards served also as instrument of the government to squeeze smallholder producers (Eicher and Baker 1982) through low producer prices and depressed or relaxed currency controls. In the past the surplus went directly into state coffers through investment in sectors like manufacturing, hotels and tourism and large-scale commercial farming. In this context one could rightly invoke Michael Lipton's notion of *'urban bias'* to explain the persistence of rural poverty. As Eicher and Baker once put it the manipulation of agricultural prices served as a standard technique to influence the level and composition of agricultural production and the transfer of the surplus to urban centres. To that extent to date depressed producer prices explain the widening gap between rural and urban incomes. Unfortunately depressed food prices have many negative effects among which are: reduced incentive to produce more food and export crops, reduced ability of the government to establish and maintain food reserves and reduced employment opportunities in farming, processing and rural industries.

Case studies of ADMARC and COCOBOD

For Malawi, prior to the liberalization of the farming sector in the late 1980s and through the 1990s, smallholder producers were ruthlessly exploited. They were obliged to sell to ADMARC at very low prices while estate owners were allowed to sell individually. ADMARC made enormous gain out of it but the profits could not trickle down to the small-scale producers. Profits ended up in the central treasury through which it was used to further the interests of the ruling political party henchmen. Similar arrangements have been reported for Ghana where COCOBOD used to pay cocoa farmers barely 40% of the world price in the 1970s and 1980s. In the mid-1990s when cocoa prices on the world market went up COCOBOD continued to pay farmers about 50% of the international market price. As Swift (1998) observed low farm gate prices made cocoa farmers hopeless, some left the land and many became absentee city dwellers. The irony is that the actual dynamics of price squeeze are not straight forward as the cases of ADMARC and COCOBOD suggest.

At the surface of it price squeeze arises from the fact that agricultural production is linked in one way or another to the world market. The link manifests itself in marketing linkages involving both farm inputs (farm equipment, fertilizer and seeds, pesticides) and farm outputs. Both the smallholder and large-scale producers tend to be victims since prices of farm inputs tend to increase at a higher rate than prices of agricultural output. This is generally true for all prices of raw materials as opposed to prices of associated finished products. The extraction of surplus from the smallholder producers follows a particular pattern. Bienefeld (1986) had observed that surplus extraction from agriculture is more severe in poor countries because the political importance of cheap food policies is relatively greater. Extraction is also greater where rural producers are less powerful, as is the situation of the majority of smallholder producers in Malawi. Surplus is easier to extract from export crops such as tobacco, tea, coffee, cotton, paprika and sugar, since their marketing tends to be easier to control. Further, surplus extraction is likely to be more intense when the economy has no access to significant amounts of surplus from alternative sources, for example, tourism, manufacturing, minerals and mining, remittances and telecommunications. Often, palliative transfers of resources to the rural areas are tried via small-scale to large-scale projects and discretionary subsidies like TIP. Subsidy is often favoured over higher producer prices because it can be directed to specific and identifiable groups on discretionary and sufficiently visible basis and can be exploited quite easily to win political mileage given the tendency of policy makers in poor countries to promote policies that serve narrow self-interest rather than public interest. Even where public interests are

100

served there is bound to be disguised self-interests as various analyses of the Botswana Meat Commission (BMC) show.

Case study of the Botswana Meat Commission
In the 1970s through the 1990s BMC's beef exports to Europe attracted prices higher than average world prices. Higher prices earned from beef exports trickled down to the farmers through the system of bonuses (Fidzani et al 1996; Hesselberg 1985; Government of Botswana 1991). In this respect the BMC could be considered an exception to the rule. How can we explain the practice of bonuses in the light of Bienefeld's pattern of extraction of surplus from small-scale producers? Certainly Botswana's socioeconomic situation confirms Bienefeld's pattern. The importance of agriculture in the economy of Botswana has declined over the decades (Selolwane 1992). The agricultural share of the national gross domestic product declined from 40% at independence to 3% in 1990s (Government of Botswana 1991, 1997). Agriculture is like a lagging sector and among reasonable policy makers it would be logical not to tax beef producers heavily. Yet, on the problems to Botswana's rural economy and agriculture, Selolwane (1992) bemoaned class interests of policy makers which approximates Bienefeld's 'group interests'. The skewed distribution of cattle ownership in Botswana has been well documented (Hesselberg 1985; Government of Botswana 1997) and the share of BMC's profits follows the same pattern. The concentration of cattle is particularly pronounced among the very few big farmers. As early as 1981, nineteen cattle farms had 60% of the total national herd. The herd sizes were on average 10 000 and these big cattle owners were chiefs or relatives to chiefs, a reflection of 'initial

101

inequality in cause of today's inequality' (Hesselberg 1985: 182). In these circumstances, one cannot evade or shun Bienefeld's notion of the 'self-interests' of the elites. The favourable prices offered by BMC are in favour of the big cattle farmers. With regard to these basic facts Fidzani et al. (1996) noted that the assumption that all farmers are price responsive overlooks the multifariousness of cattle ownership in Botswana. It creates opportunity of accumulation of which the bigger farmers alone can take advantage. Moreover, as Hesselberg (1985)) observed the inequalities in rural areas are amplified by policy bias towards the cattle sector in which the elite are the major beneficiaries.

Price squeeze may take other dimensions, for example, in relation to food imports, food aid, disparities in rural- urban prices of goods and services and differential resource endowments between the rural rich and poor households. An uncontrolled import of cheap agricultural commodities to supplement food shortage is an indirect way of squeezing producer prices. A case in point is the low price for food crops like maize associated with the flooding of the market with cheap food imports or food brought in and distributed by national and international organizations to vulnerable population. An example is the case of Kenya and Tanzania where maize food aid for Somali and Rwandan refugees ended up in the market competing with locally produced food. Somali and Rwandan refugees did not like maize so they ended up selling it cheaply to buy rice and other items. At one time in the 1990s the price of maize in Tanzania dropped from 10 000 Shillings per 100Kg to 3 000 Shillings following an influx of maize aid (Nayaran 1997). Other than the flooding of the market with imports or food aid, lack of roads or efficient transport system imply that rural smallholder producers have to sell their commodities in the village at very low prices. In Tanzania, during the 1993 – 4 harvest one bag of maize sold at 3 600 shillings in the village and 6 000 Shillings in the towns. A tin of beans went for 1 000 Shillings in the village and 2 500 Shillings in town (Nayaran 1997).

Problems of low prices and disparities between rural-urban prices do not have the same effect on all rural households. The rich households have greater advantage over the poor households as Nayaran demonstrated in relation to marketing of cotton in Tanzania in the 1990s. When the marketing of cotton became a problem rich farm households moved quickly out of cotton to cashew production. The different abilities of the rich and the poor to take advantage of markets were reflected by where they also sold their produce. The rich who would deal in large quantities had greater access to transport facilities and sold their produce to private traders and in towns, while the poor sold through local markets, other farmers, cooperatives and to private traders. Rich farmers negotiated and set prices while the poor dealing in small quantities and lacking in staying power to bargain for better prices accepted to sell at lower prices. As a norm 'the rich were those who set prices' and 'the poor as those who are forced to accept the prices set by others' (Nayaran 1997:45).

Lack of and inappropriately targeted subsidies and higher levels of poverty compelled households to sell products soon after harvest when prices were relatively low and to buy back food later when prices are high. This is a serious challenge where households need cash urgently to settle debts, purchase essential supplies, or meet unexpected emergency such as medical or funeral costs. Crops may be sold 'green' before harvest at substantial discount. The following statement by a poor woman drawn from Bernstein (1992b: 19) is illustrative of this phenomenon:

> 'We had to borrow money to eat. Sometimes neighbours would lend us money without interest, but we often had to sell our rice before the harvest. Moneylenders would pay us in advance, and take our rice at half the market price'.

Pellekaan and Hartnett summed up well the marketing contradiction as follows: 'inadequate access to markets for goods and services caused by the poor's remote geographical location, inadequate rural roads, ineffective communication and the small volume and seasonality of the poor's labour services and production means that rural producers are severely at a disadvantage' (Pellekaan and Hartnett 2000:37). The paradox is that such precariousness is sometimes tolerated and exacerbated by the state's need to secure the well-being of and to placate urban consumers as well as gain urban political support through direct and indirect controls on rising food prices.

Direct controls are achieved through pre-set low minimum farm gate prices and subsidies that make the rural producers think they are producing cheaply. Indirectly, the state tolerates trade malpractices by the private traders who offer to buy farm produce at low prices or who use false weights and measures. Quite often many private traders operating in this manner have connections to ruling political parties. Such traders are in some cases sponsors of political parties in power and are more often than not used as conduits to siphon state resources through dubious contracts with the state. Low food prices for urban consumers means low incomes for farmers both male and female farmers. The burden of very low producer prices is felt most by the female producers for reasons related to challenges of access to distant markets.[7] The precarious situation of women and female-headed households in agriculture was recently summarized as follows:

> The majority of women are small-holders producing on a very small-scale and relatively unaffected by developments in the use of improved tools and seeds, and yields are highly determined by the weather. Their involvement in agricultural production is often a struggle to first provide enough for their households. This does not encourage savings against future consumption, against economic shocks and other hazards. (Sikod 2007:64)

With very few opportunities for raising incomes low producer prices constitute an extra burden, which is sometimes a barrier to high end technology.

Appropriate technology

In a classical study of rural stagnation Clifford Geertz (1963) argued that Indonesian's reluctance to adopt technological change during the 1950s led to stagnation in production prior to the 1960s, a phenomenon he termed 'agricultural involution'. In other words, involution could be avoided by adoption of appropriate technology. Appropriate technology affords capacity to overcome production and post-harvest bottlenecks. Sometimes appropriateness may relate to social power relations, that is, who has the power to define a technological problem and therefore to prescribe the solution. Taking cognizance of this situation Wilson (1990) noted that appropriate technology is one which gives control to individuals and communities at local level rather than to the technocrats in government or to private enterprises.

Criteria for defining the appropriateness of technology includes the extent to which it conforms to or does not disrupt the cultural fabric; the extent to which the operation and maintenance can be done locally; the extent to which the technology uses locally available resources, its environmental friendliness, its flexibility, and its gender inclusiveness. Appropriate technology could be community specific or simply put appropriate to a particular area and culture, given that it accords with the populist vision of small-scale producers having a large measure of control of the technology (Wilson 1990). Questions are ever raised on the potential contribution of small-scale 'appropriate technology' to raising productive capacities, to ensuring economic development and permanent improvement in well-being. It would appear that much of agricultural technology on the market in Malawi does not meet the criteria of appropriateness. Existing traditional tools like the hoe, sickle and machete (*panga*) knife appear to be appropriate from the point of simplicity, durability, reliability and cost. The desirability of technological change cannot be overemphasized given that much of what constitute traditional

106

technologies represents the status quo or a state of technological equilibrium and technological fossilization.

Making and supplying a million new hoes, sickles, watering cans and even treadle pumps cannot increase agricultural productivity in the absence of other changes, nor will it result in increases in gainful employment. Similarly, free or subsidized fertilizer will not make households food secure where rainfall and temperature patterns are not ideal, or where producers face serious constraints with respect to inadequate land holdings. In early 2000s Malawian government tried at expand irrigated land through the distribution of 250 treadle pumps to each one of the 193 constituencies. Treadle pump is an example of technologies that appear appropriate but have limited potential to revolutionize the way farming is carried out even at household level. Its adoption is not as big as anticipated partly because farmers are selective when it comes to adoption of technology. Technologies, which do not meet the farmers' needs, capacity and interests, are less likely to be adopted just like those involving high initial costs and those that conflict with and do not contribute to household welfare objectives. It has been suggested that men and women who have acquired and use treadle pumps are often too tired after hours of peddling the pump. Some men fail to perform in bed to the satisfaction of the spouse. Hence, although use of treadle pumps can contribute to food availability, which is a requirement for happy marriages, by disenabling men the technology can be a source of marital instability and unfaithful patterns in some instances. It follows also that research and development of new agricultural technologies should be directed towards meeting farmer's objectives and overcoming existing constraints as well as promotion of marital ties. Where it is feasible emphasis should be on building on the indigenous technologies that are already in use, and on sound understanding of the smallholder farmers' production rationality and capacity. Such knowledge can be obtained from the farmers themselves through participatory processes.

Otherwise, as Warburton (1990) argued, it is meaningless to provide tractors, for example, to people who have not been shown how to use them and more importantly people who do not know how to repair them when they break down or where spare parts may be unavailable locally. Certainly, governments have a big role in the provision and adoption of appropriate technology.[8] Recently, the need and demand for appropriate technology has been enhanced by the challenge of climate change. Already, a great deal of money, time and effort has been allocated to understanding this phenomenon, which is also a reflection of its seriousness.

Appropriate technologies will be required to cushion farmers against extremes of adverse and variable weather regimes, at least to guarantee some level of sustainable food supply. Combating effects of climate change will require investments in technologies (machinery, fuel, water, fertilizer, foodstuff, and seeds), technical information (training and breeding), insurance (fire, accident, and life), medical (vaccines), and relief service to support adaptation or mitigation of the effects of climate change. Better organisation of farmers could go a long way towards improving the situation of poor resource and technologically underprivileged given that access to modern technology, appropriate technology inclusive, in the developing world is quite low largely as a result

108

of lack of capital, skills and knowledge, all of which could be mobilized if better farmer organization was pursued with vigour. The challenges to expanding green revolution technology could be partly ameliorated by better farmer organization and through the institution of farmer cooperatives.

Green revolution as appropriate technology

The green revolution started in parts of Asia and Latin America (Mexico in particular) where the introduction of high yielding varieties (HYV) without guaranteed access to complimentary inputs like irrigation, fertilizer, insecticides, credit and agricultural extension services favoured a small minority of large land holders and furthered the impoverishment of the rural poor. Large land owners with disproportionate access to complimentary inputs and support services gained competitive advantage over smallholders, consequently driving them out of the market (Todaro 1992). In Africa government action to subsidize interests rates for agricultural credit have in some cases resulted in a transfer of government resources to large and male farmers with very little credit available to small farmers who are forced to turn to the money lenders (Stevens 1977; Todaro 1992) The inevitable though unintentional result has been further widening of the gap between the rich and the poor or the large-scale and the smallholder producers' access to green revolution technology.

Instances and experiences in Asia reveal stark gender based inequalities. The introduction of rice mills in Java and Korea displaced women from the traditional tasks in favour of men (Bandarage 1984). As Asoka Bandarage noted the benefits of the green revolution accrued to men because the handing of technology to men left women with few opportunities of earning a living. Earlier writings, Feder (1976) for instance, aptly summed up the direct results of the green revolution noting that it sharply increased concentration of land ownership, contributed to massive dispossession of smallholders, proliferation of landless workers, heightened rural unemployment, poverty, hunger and increased domination of the multinational interests over production and distribution of agricultural products and inputs. Another interesting analysis of the effects of the Green revolution is provided by Huw Jones (1990:52) and it reads:

> 'Even where food production per capita has increased partly through increased irrigation and the adoption of Green Revolution high-yielding cereals, there is no assurance that the bulk of the population has benefited nutritionally. It has been widely alleged that the Green Revolution has benefited a small, politically powerful elite of large, rich farmers at the expense of the majority of peasants who are unable to afford, and sometimes to understand, the package of fertilizers, pesticides and water input necessary for the successful adoption of new crop varieties. Particularly in Latin America, technological transformation of agriculture has led to an increasing concentration of land ownership and maldistribution of agricultural income that in turn produces increasing pauperization and malnutrition in the majority of the rural population'.

Writing mainly for India, rising rural incomes from green revolution technologies occurred at a time when rural poverty was rising due to twin processes (Bardhan 1984). First, the adoption of labour displacing machinery, which meant thousands of agricultural labourers lost their jobs and therefore incomes. The adoption of machinery, however, led to increased yields due to efficiency and speed at which activities could be performed. Since then, of particular importance has been speedy accomplishment of tasks because the green revolution technologies permit double to triple cropping. The second process is slow growth in wage rates accompanied by price rises for agricultural commodities. This process meant that rural people had to pay more for food resulting into little cash for other needs like clothing, health care and education. The most surprising aspect is, however, that growth in agricultural productivity did not lead to a decline in food prices as the law of demand and supply states. This occurred because of and was reinforced by food exports, which meant low supply of food on the domestic market. Above all the state failed to stimulate adequate growth of infrastructure-transportation, water resources, storage facilities and credit institutions, all of which are necessary to support production, the marketing and accessibility cum availability of food.

Success in agricultural cooperation depends on having informed or educated farmers with strong spirit of common purpose. Where the farmers are illiterate and ignorant they risk either being cheated by the few individuals capable of managing the cooperative on their behalf or if government is involved in running the cooperatives for the farmers, the farmers may lack sense of ownership and so perceive cooperatives as organs of the government (Lowe 1986). Given the advantages mentioned already, one would wonder at why cooperatives have not been a successful in Malawi. The explanation could be linked to the low literacy rates in rural areas which mean farmers are ignorant of the benefits of cooperation. However, it needs noting also that traditional forms of power and mutual support that are not conducive to the primary goal of enhancing efficiency have found ground and new space of articulation in cooperatives. This is true where members in farming cooperatives incorporate mutual support during funerals, initiation and wedding ceremonies. Good as it may sound as a means towards formation of social capital, eventually good members in farming cooperative become those who are available for the social functions not those who are most effective in managing their time and other resources to enhance agricultural production.

In some cases, however, the problem lies with government agricultural policies. As Mafeje (1992) once put it the need to extract surplus underlie African governments' distrust of cooperatives and the minimum level of support accorded to autonomous smallholder farmer organizations. No wonder that wherever cooperative farming has been encouraged by governments, for example, under Tanzania's villagization programme, cooperatives were strictly monitored and autonomous activities were curtailed or directed to meet government demands to produce particular export crops (Lyimo 1999). Under such conditions farmers would consider social capital as the only legitimate expression of local initiative.

Effects of commercialization of smallholder agriculture

Commercialization of small-scale production is necessary if agricultural growth is to take place. Agriculture both large and small scale should contribute to the creation of the home market that is essential for import substitution industry and for export oriented industry. For Harris such change is required involving transformation in the total system of relationships, including transformation of social, cultural, technological relations and a range of processes that affect and contribute to agricultural production (Harris 1982) allowing the agricultural producers to realize full potential to generate and release in sufficient quantity and on reasonable terms a surplus. For Michael Lipton, however, economic growth is of secondary importance to the need to reduce poverty (Lipton 1974) and satisfy domestic demand for food. It follows that if agriculture is neglected and supplies of food and raw materials are not forthcoming, industrialization could not flourish.

An expanding agricultural sector can earn foreign exchange through exports to pay for imported capital equipment and essential raw materials. Further, a rapidly growing agricultural sector can be a source of savings for investment and financing social overhead capital like roads, water, electricity, and health and education (Singh 1999). A prosperous agriculture can also provide benefits including higher rural incomes that are essential if national demand for locally made industrial products is to grow (see table 5.2).

Table 5.2 The benefits of agricultural growth

Level	Benefits
Farm economy	1) Higher incomes for farmers, including smallholders. 2) More employment on-farm as labour demand rises per hectare, the area cultivated expands, or frequency of cropping increases. 3) Rise in farm wage rates
Rural economy	1) More jobs in agriculture and food chain upstream and downstream off farm 2) More jobs or higher incomes in non-farm economy as farmers and farm labourers spend additional incomes 3) Increased jobs and incomes in rural economy allow better nutrition, better health and increased investment in education amongst rural population. Lead directly to improved welfare, and indirectly to higher labour productivity 4) More local tax revenues generated and demand for better infrastructure- roads, power supplies, and communications. Leads to second-round effects promoting rural economy. 5) Linkages in production chain generate trust and information, build social capital and facilitate non-farm investment. 6) Reduced prices of food for rural inhabitants who buy in food net.
National economy	1) Reduced prices of food and raw materials raises wages of urban poor, reduce wage costs of non-farm sectors.

	2) Generation of savings and taxes from farming allows investment in on-farm sector, creating jobs and incomes in other sectors. 3) Earning of foreign exchange allows import of capital goods and essential inputs for non-farm production 4) Release of farm labour allows production in other sectors.

Source: Lrz et al (2001)

Concluding reflections

There are already indications that when prospects for farm profits are good, small-scale farmers innovate, adopt technologies, improve existing practices or increase production (Eicher and Baker 1982; Low 1986; Bernstein 1992) even without direct state stimuli or coercion. However, when prospects for some profit are rather remote smallholder farmers become less innovative even where state subsidies are provided. A multi-pronged approach is required involving six *in*s: *in*centives to the farmers in the form of better prices, *in*puts, *in*novation (technology), *in*formation that facilitates diffusion of technology through extension services, *in*frastructure and *in*stitutions that provide credit, marketing and land reforms (Streeten 1995:64). Sustainable progress would require investment in population control measures, the creation of alternative rural employment opportunities, and addressing the land question.

Notes

[1] Buell identifies the source as Nineteenth Annual Report, 1923, British Cotton Growing association, Manchester, p. 29.

[2] In some countries peasant production competed well with the plantation farming of coffee in Ivory Coast and in Tanganyika. Chaga cultivators in the Mount Kilimanjaro foothills emerged as the most successful Africa farmers producing the best coffee. In Uganda, low world prices for cotton in the 1920s ruined large scale farmers but peasant production survived well (Hull 1980).

[3] What was available for the native farmer by way of extension in the late 1940s and 1950s were draconian soil and water conservation measures. Those reluctant to follow recommended practices had their crops destroyed and some farmers were imprisoned. The severely of conservation measures led to resentment of colonial rule and it appears that the draconian measures were eventually exploited by the nationalist movement in the 1950s, the Nyasaland African Congress (NAC). Thereafter an alternative mode of extension implemented by the colonial government was the ill-conceived and ill-timed master farmer model. Master farmers as Nambote observed were native farmers but who were in many respects settler farmers incarnate as they were prominent in a way and quite influential in a particular area. The white farmers in black skin were provided seeds, fertilizer, implements such as ploughs and advisory services. The assumption was that innovations would then trickle to neighboring farmers through demonstration effect. On attaining independence in 1964 the concept of master farmer was abolished without carefully analysis and consideration of its benefits (see Nambote 1998).

[4] ADMARC taxed the smallholder sector and transferred the resources realized to the estate sector and companies directly controlled by the head of state. ADMARC cross-subsidized smallholder maize production but on the other hand it offered guaranteed prices to the small holder farmers often fixed barely 20% of the border or export prices (Chirwa et al. 2006; Harrigan 1991). Later in the 1970s IRDPs were integrated into the nation-wide National Rural Development Programme (NRDP), which was accompanied by the creation of eight Agricultural Development Divisions (ADDs), fertilizer subsidies to smallholder farmers and credit.

[5] Malawi Economic Justice Network (MEJN) 'How Priority Poverty Expenditures are Implemented' Civil Society Agriculture Network (CISANET) Civil Society Budget Monitoring 2002/2003.

[6] In general the process of selection was widely viewed by community members as having been unfair and biased, and this in turn led to resentment towards village heads. Some Village headmen were beaten, while other people feared being bewitched. In those villages where the selection process was considered fair, transparent and public, the divisions were kept to a minimum. In addition, the programme had negative impacts on political and development activities at village level where many people left out vowed not to participate in local elections; and some people refused to take part in community development work thereafter (Lawson et al. 2001). Lawson and others reported that in some cases villagers referred to themselves in terms such as *'we are all poor here'*, which can be read as resistance to state sponsored effort to impose social categories. Attempts to target along disadvantaged social categories such as orphans and the aged could also undermine efforts to poverty target since such categories are also not neatly correlated with poverty. However, the major challenge to be noted in many places is nepotism, which is the tendency to favour family, relatives and friends

[7] The World Bank's *World Development Report, Poverty in the 1990s* cited a village study in India's Uttar Pradesh state where the most disadvantaged groups were landless casual labourers who could not secure work on regular basis and households *without an able-bodied male* (World Bank 1990:33). In 1983 – 4, all households with both these characteristics were found to be poor.

[8] This was demonstrated by Julius Nyerere, former resident of Tanzania and advocate of appropriate technology. One of his policy driven statements supporting appropriate technology read: 'Our future lies in the development of our agriculture and in the development of our rural areas. But because we are seeking to grow from our own roots and to preserve that which is valuable in our traditional past, we have also to stop thinking in terms of massive agricultural mechanization. We have, instead to think in terms of development through improvement of the tools we now use, and through the growth of cooperative systems of production. Instead of aiming at large farms using tractors and other modern equipment and employing agricultural labourers, we should be aiming at ox-ploughs all over the country. The *jembe* will have to be eliminated by the ox-plough before the latter can be eliminated by the tractor. We cannot hope to eliminate the *jembe* by the tractor. Instead of thinking about providing each

farmer with his own lorry, we should consider the usefulness of ox-drawn carts, which could be made within the country and which are appropriate both to our roads and to the loads which each farmer is likely to have. Instead of aerial spraying of crops with insecticide, we should use hand pumps. In other words, we have to think in terms of what is available, or can be made available at comparatively small cost, and which can be operated by the people. By moving into the future along this path, we can avoid massive social disruption and human suffering' (White 1973:43 - 4).

Chapter Six

Commodification of customary land relations in peri-urban villages

This chapter is dedicated to examination of commodification of customary land in peri-urban villages. The process involves customary landholders playing the role of land sellers, the buyers, and persons holding traditional rank of village head and intermediaries or agents. The transactions entail permanent alienation of land and there is no attempt to disguise the process either as involving gifting of land or short term rent. Pertinent issues are how and why attitudes and practices are evolving, and how the sellers and buyers represent themselves in the course of attributing exchangeability and interchangeability between land and money. The practice undermines land rights of customary landholders and so feeds into the uncertain livelihood and anchor the vulnerability of the land sellers. The practice shows very well one facet of underdevelopment from within. It explains perceptions regarding the changing value of land and more broadly deagrarianization in peri-urban villages.

The changing value of land

Recent interest on land issues in sub-Saharan Africa is mixed up with large scale foreign land acquisitions,[1] associated with the production of food and biofuels for export markets in the rich nations. Against the soaring global food and fuel prices, an interesting contradiction is that recent large scale land acquisitions raise a fundamental question about land rights and security of tenure for local populations. In a general sense the fear is that, also informed by historical precedents, many local populations might endure forced eviction, involuntary relocation to make way for plantations or exploited as labourers or out-growers. For southern Africa, there are concerns related to past experiences like recent demands for land restitution in South Africa (James 2007) or land governance and sovereignty in Zimbabwe (Moyo 2010).

In Malawi the discourse on large scale and foreign land acquisitions is slowly gaining ground. Such a discourse eclipses ongoing small-scale acquisitions of customary land in peri-urban villages. The scale at which the selling of customary land is occurring makes it a significant development challenge considering also the social and governance structures that are implicated. Traditional chiefs, the executive and other arms of the state are similarly implicated in the process as they go about everyday business of legislating and interpreting and enforcing law whenever disputes arise.

What is apparent is the changing value attached to land. Writing about this aspect in the context of Lagos between 1760 and 1900, Mann (2007) observed that on top of the traditional use values, land and housing eventually acquired functions such as collateral for credit, source of rental income and an object of speculative investment over and above the 'traditional' values of it being a place of domestic shelter, livelihood and centre of individual and family religious, social, and political activity. Then the new opportunities emerged first within the town but over time spread to rural areas stimulating the scramble for land and landed property, which also led to dramatic increase in the value of land and the demand for title for land. In the context of this chapter commodification is a process whereby customary land becomes a commodity or object of economic value (Appadurai 1986:3).

The nature of commodities has been a subject of theoretical debate in terms of what commodities embody. Key ideas include the dichotomous association of commodities with gifts, exchangeability and objectification, use value versus exchange-value, and alienability (Appadurai 1986; Benediktsson 2002). Customary land that is sold or bought becomes a part commodity and its personality is split into use and exchange values. Appadurai's notion of 'social life of things' suggests that the same item could be both a commodity and a gift in different social and historical contexts of exchange and interaction. The ambiguity is that things are commodified to the extent that access is determined by the market, and decommodified to the extent that access is determined by criteria other than ability to pay, including need and social relationships. The commodification of customary land, defined narrowly as monetization of land relations, does not mean that land circulates as other commodities or gifts would, but that it is nevertheless subject to 'exchange-value calculations' and 'increasing market mentality' (Benediktsson 2002:31). Commodification would in a broader sense incorporate the practice of thinking about daily interactions as if they were transactions. The ambivalence is that besides the potential tension between use and exchange values land is often caught in the dilemma of state law on land versus customary law on land, both of which seek to regulate its use or non-use, exchange and alienability or non-alienability. This chapter looks into the practice in order to locate growing livelihood insecurity and uncertainty experienced by peri-urban communities as a result of peri-urbanization and objectification of peri-urban customary land. It shows that despite everyday expectations by land sellers, commodification of customary land is not decisive step towards attaining livelihood security. To appreciate the dynamics involved this chapter will examine the process of commodification of customary land in peri-urban villages, associated socio-economic transformations and how the actors grapple with uncertainties and insecurities that ensue.

Customary land in perspective

Customary land is treated as a resource with use and sometimes symbolic value; yet it is assumed that it cannot be alienated or sold[2] or as Mitzi Goheen put it, disposed of as a 'resource with a cash value assigned to its use and ownership' (Goheen 1992:390). In reality, what is presented as custom, the unwritten law or beliefs or social patterns and practices established by long usage and recognized as legitimate within particular cultural contexts, is a set of norms, but how it is put into practice and the relations to effective land tenure tends to be different. Ongoing practices suggest that conventions on land either as custom or law are often broken.

By its nature the commodification of customary land may include renting and swapping of fields, though in renting and swapping, land is not sold or bought. For some years, many villagers have been renting out fields and also selling land at bargain prices and at other times for large amounts of money. Apparently, poverty and inequality define contours of interactions in most land relations. Yet, one of the conventional arguments is that since the economic liberalizations of the 1980s many farming populations in peri-urban zones have had to decide whether to sell land or not, and whether to leave farming or not; a trend few would have been prepared to contemplate decades earlier (Lentz 2007). In Malawi, like many sub-Sahara African countries, selling of customary land takes place mostly in peri-urban villages, though many peri-urban villagers dependent on smallholder cultivation claim to be constrained by shortage of arable land, besides other serious challenges such as high prices of farm inputs and lack of alternative and gainful employment opportunities.

Selling customary land raises questions of significant interest because the right to own it is not ordinarily vested in the individual person but in groups to which individuals belong. The group may include the family, the lineage, the clan and the village under hereditary leadership of the village head or chief. In practice the right to use land in perpetuity is vested in individual person and so landholdings are worked individually (or by individual families) rather than collectively by the community. At the level of facts, individuals (or families) own and control land, while at the level of ideas it is the group which controls it (Kandawire 1977). Sometimes this distinction is not clear and consistently made; given also the lack of clearly defined boundaries between land tenure, kinship, social obligation, the family and the economy. The question becomes does the shift from a resource to a commodity also suggest shifts from more communal to more individualized forms of tenure or acceptance of the idea that individuals rather than kin groups have power to control and even dispose land.

Unlike registered land, which is surveyed, mapped and set up for sale or purchase, customary land comprises of untitled fields or gardens that are often irregular in shape, a reflection of random, culturally bound fragmentation characteristic of subdivision of land as successive generations pass on gardens received from previous generations. These processes and practices happen unregulated by the state. The people buying up the fields take advantage of relatively lower land prices, the poverty or ignorance of the sellers, and also their own greater wealth compared to land sellers. Later, some buyers regularize ownership by applying for lease with the state. As peri-urban fields are absorbed or become hives of construction for residential and commercial uses, questions related to who owns the land, who controls it and how it might be transferred further become more fluid and sometimes contested. Peri-urban villages become arenas of both conflict and change given that such transactions make the land seller immediately or ultimately landless. Apparently, most of the land sellers cannot compete with outsiders with a formal job and a more stable source of income (Ubink 2006). The state and sometimes traditional leaders are slow to act and rarely see the situation as irreversibly changing, and oftentimes hold normative positions about customary law on land and pre-existing social relations as unchanging. The view that customary law is ancient and unchallengeable, retaining its principles through long periods of time, its origins lost in the mists of antiquity, has been challenged and in other instances discarded altogether. Customary laws are changing and have been subject to constant change in the pre-colonial past (Gluckman 1969:9; Lawson 1997)

Locating the peri-urban

The term peri-urban refers to intermediate spaces or zones in transition between rural and urban spaces for which other descriptive terms are 'rurban', 'suburban', 'urban fringe', 'urban periphery', 'perirural', etc. Perceived in relation to outward expansion of the urban zone into the rural zone, it is often associated with the spread of urban populations and developments, though population growth is not the only reason for the growth of peri-urban settlements. The dynamics that determine peri-urban growth involve a number of dimensions that may include land regulation and taxation, infrastructure and housing policies of the state. Quite often the administrative boundaries marking the rural-urban divide symbolize inconsistent representation of reality. Simone suggested that the operations in peri-urban appear to be simply reassertion of rural ways or parodies of urban practices, but without really being either (Simone 1998). This perception embodies modern assumptions about the use and political control of space. Often peri-urban settlers rarely consider themselves and they do not try to live like ordinary villagers.

Commodification of customary land as a process

In the first place land is sold by the customary owners or the customary users in legal parlance, from those with traditional rank and those without, who might be selling customary land for the first time or those who might have bought the land and are therefore reselling. On their part village headmen and headwomen grant consent. The village head is then a third party whose role is sometimes portrayed dismissively as that of the witness. Yet, after the village head has granted consent, it is often represented as if the village headman or headwoman allocated the land. Therefore the language used disguises the transaction as involving redistribution of land.

To a certain degree the transactions are ambiguous and 'informal', where informality is not about illegality of the transactions but more fundamentally about the agency and intentionality of the actors. The notion of informality is useful precisely because of its ambiguity. It is used in two quite different senses that peri-urban land transactions bring into relation. It distinguishes ordinary practices from 'formal' practices. Being formal means following procedures set by the state and in that sense the object could be leased or registered land. In the second sense, being informal draws attention to the intentionality of the actors. Further, informality implicates how government officials dealing with land, especially in relation to those seeking to lease customary land operate. If the applicant indicates on the lease application form that he or she bought customary land from a village headman or a chief, for example, they would normally be advised to indicate that the village headman or chief allocated the land for free.

Shifting attitudes towards the selling of land

The act of selling and buying land is becoming the major way of transferring and acquiring peri-urban land. To some degree the processes signify the impact of growing peri-urbanization and the gradual and too often unintended and spontaneous integration of the peri-urban land into objectified urban space. The selling and buying of customary land links the sellers and the buyers and both become symbolically attached to or disassociated with it in a new way. This idea of being attached or disassociated with the land is the essence of objectification. The idea of objectification is rooted in the writings of Hegel as Phillip Vannini suggests, for Hegel objectification refers to 'the process whereby human beings undertake a double process of separation first and re-appropriation later of the material world' (Vannini 2009b:22). Critical to objectification of customary land are changing attitudes towards customary land, uncertain rural livelihood security and the changing perceptions on general scarcity value of land.

Many peri-urban villagers subscribe to the view that in the past customary land in peri-urban villages could be allocated and reallocated free of charge by village headmen or resident families to new comers and strangers (*obwera*) or those who begged for it (*opempha malo*). Then, what mattered most were factors such as affiliation to the village, the ethnic group and declaration of allegiance, which were followed by some offer of some valuables in return (gift), for example a chicken (*nkhuku*), piece of cloth (*chilundu*) or oftentimes a pot of beer (*chipanda cha mowa*) usually provided after a growing season. Marcel Mauss' treatise on reciprocity emphasizes that 'gifts' entail the right to receive and the obligation to reciprocate or as Jomo Kenyatta put it the principle of 'give and take' (Kenyatta 1971:19). In many cases such exchange helps to create webs of relationships based on mutual obligations, which also function as safety nets for people with few economic resources, insufficient state welfare benefits or limited access to goods and services.

Of late these procedures are no longer considered sufficient. Land has acquired new value, and there is an increase in the number of people willing to sell or buy it. Some sellers regard the selling of land as a form of business, hence the prominence of intermediaries and agents. Besides rising demand many villagers also associate the selling of land to the rise in levels of poverty, a challenge that does not spare the village heads. For some village heads, the selling of land is a new form of business. The situation in the peri-urban villages in peri-urban Malawi, Blantyre in particular, is therefore similar to that observed by Vele (1978) in Papua New Guinea where some people acquired land for almost free in the late 1960s but by the end of the 1970s most land transactions involved cash payments. Vele reported that land holders' wish to earn some money had become the driving force. Yet, as much as the commodification of land could be situated in the changing requirements for cash income, some peri-urban villagers claimed that it was not solely the desire for money that made them sell land, rather they also perceived the transactions as one way of extending generosity and hospitality which obliged those with extra land to offer it to those in need and who could put it to efficient use (Kaitilla 1999 for a similar point). Reflecting on peri-urban land transactions in Malawi; these three factors: the availability of land, the demand for land and the need for cash income are complementary forces.

The irony of selling land is that in the long run it increases pressure on land. Often, selling land does not correlate with having excess landholding, given also that few families have excess land due to growing pressure on land reported in the previous chapter. The dilemma of surrendering land to outsiders relates to the question of reconciling the use value and exchange value.[3] A similar position is made with additional layer of precision for the Luo where Shipton (1992) observed broad scepticism about selling land although the influence of pro-market ideas acquired through trade, travel, and schooling have led to some shift in the position that deemed it betrayal to alienate ancestral land for money.[4] For these reasons, in addition to the factors mentioned above, the commodification of land reflects increasing contact between the customary land holders and the market economies, though its form might also reflect the inability to defend legitimate rights (Alexander and Alexander 1995) as land becomes scarce.

Reselling of customary land is as common as selling. Selling takes effect on ancestral or inherited land while reselling is associated with purchased or privately acquired land. Hence selling and reselling highlight the contrast between personally acquired and inherited or ancestral property in land and one depends on and follows the other. A fundamental feature of reselling land is that it allows the seller to take advantage of the changing dynamics in the pricing of land. Apparently, land tends to increase in value beyond the value of profits one can gain by using it for farming purposes. For example, land values might rise relative to the rise in demand due to growing population density, the addition of public infrastructure (including water, electricity and transportation infrastructure), or the emergence of new land uses besides agriculture. Often where addition of public infrastructure is the driving force, the situation would normally reflect cumulative developments other than planned development by the state. In other words, peri-urban development may suffer from lack of coordinated planning and provision of amenities.

The general perception is that all the land buyers hail from the city, which is an incorrect representation of the overall situation. Even some local villagers are also involved in the buying of land. Some local villagers buy land for farming purposes and this is common for those who are in land scarce situation. People buying land for this reason are few in number given that prices of land in the villages closer to the city are often very high and generally unaffordable to a majority of local peri-urban villagers.

For many land buyers when they buy land and then build houses they claim that they are now settled or established (*kukhazikika*). Multiple acquisition of land, in different parts of the city or peri-urban villages is considered a significant milestone given that land has become an object of accumulation over and above its use as a means of subsistence.

Impacts on agrarian way of life

The decision to sell or resell land is often linked to financial problems experienced by the landholder, sometimes made when the customary landholding units realize that they cannot develop the land as they would want to or as others close by are eventually doing. For some peri-urban customary landholder, sometimes the wish is to buy land elsewhere far from the city where they could restart or continue with subsistence farming. As land prices tend to be relatively lower with increasing distance from the city, the land that could be acquired at the same price further away from the city could be twice or three times bigger in size to the one sold in the areas closer to the city. Given the importance of land to people's livelihoods, there is a growing awareness that selling land undermines the agrarian way of life. Nonetheless the selling and buying of land offer a new way of seeing peri-urban land relations, especially how villagers have been positioning themselves recently.

On one hand being rooted in a place is no longer dependent on having long ancestral connection to that place as the transactions are eventually leading to loss of land by those with long ancestral connections to it. Also the selling of land calls into question the basic canons of customary land ownership systems, namely: that the land ultimately belongs to the community and cannot be alienated, that within the community individuals have security of tenure for the land they require for the hut or house and gardens, and that no member of a community can be without land or landless (Bohannan and Bohannan 1968; Kenyatta 1971). Those who have been relying on renting land for farming are eventually finding it difficult to find land that they can use on rent. Right of access to hills and wetlands that were once considered open access resources is sometimes considerably reduced. The socioeconomic impacts are sometimes enormous given that the loss is permanent, at least in the life time of the concerned actors.

Some peri-urban villagers are increasingly taking up various forms of *ganyu* (piece work) as the main occupation. Those without land of their own but are interested in subsistence farming acquire use rights by renting fields in villages further away from the city limits. For those who sell land close to the city in order to buy up fields away from the city, relocation is an attractive option, but many choose to stay on while cultivating recently acquired fields located some kilometres away from their normal place of residence. Straddling peri-urban and rural spaces gives them the advantage of continuing to enjoy the advantages that proximity to the city provides. Straddling facilitates occupational specialization or some form of multi-tasking.[5]

Multitasking entails combination of various material resources, including farming and non-farm sources of income. The diversity in what people can do takes different forms in different contexts and for different reasons. Multitasking is structured by a wide range of motivations, and opportunities. It is in some cases the means to enable accumulation and yet a strategy to spread risks or cope with temporary crises in other situations. Thus it is ideal as adaptive strategy to long-term declines in income or entitlements. The level of involvement in multitasking varies across individuals and family units to which they belong. In many cases the urge towards multi-tasking is strong for those who do not sufficient land holdings. Many peri-urban residents tend to be in such a state after selling all or most of their customary landholdings. Regarding the viability of multitasking, however, Brycesson (1999) noted that it weakens rather than strengthen productivity by detracting individual and households' achievement of higher agricultural productivity through the diversion of labour and capital to non-farm activities. In other words, diversification sacrifices the gains of specialization in favour of spreading risks. In this view diversified livelihoods may not provide decisive step forward, but rather a fumbling attempt to 'make do' in severely deficient economic environment.

In the final analysis as demand for peri-urban land is rising prices are also rising substantially, making it attractive for more villagers to consider selling even more land. Objectification occurs at different levels and for different mitigating reasons, but the major factors are the need for cash by the sellers and land by the buyers. The commodification of customary land highlights several important trajectories; the breakdown of intergeneration land transfers, and the growing pressure on land in response to population growth, urban sprawl and the speculation it encourages. Multitasking and diversification are contributing to erosion of an agrarian way of life at unexpected high rate and the net effect on rural development and poverty eradication could be negligible than has been thought of and represented.

Notes

[1] The trend has attracted a lot of attention, also referred to as 'the foreignisation of space' (Zoomers 2010)

[2] This position is also captured in the press release by the Ministry of Lands, Housing and Urban Development titled 'Response to the Article in Nation Newspaper (5.11.09) Entitled 'Mussa Lambasts Immigration, Lands: They Have Sold Malawi to Foreigners', *The Nation*, 16 November 2009. Mussa happened to be the minister for labour at that time.

[3] As Alexander and Alexander suggest based on research among Lehanan in Central Borneo, given a choice some villagers would prefer to retain their land for future cultivation rather than surrender it to outsiders, even in the unlikely circumstance that the compensation is generous (Alexander and Alexander 1995).

[4] Among the Luo money gained from selling inherited land for personal gain is called *mekech*, bitter or evil. Such money must be kept out of sacred spheres such as marriage payments, particularly for a marriage to a second or subsequent wife, seen increasingly as a luxury for a man. The belief is that if mixed up without being ritually purified, 'bitter money' brings sterility and death by the agency of ancestral spirits, divinity, or both – to the seller and his family and lineage (Shipton 1992: 365).

[5] Numerous studies in sub-Saharan Africa, Latin America and in transition economies of Eastern Europe in the 1990s and recently demonstrated sufficiently that individuals and families are rarely dependent on just one source of food and income, let alone solely on agriculture (Manona 2001; Scoones 1998, 2009; Zoomers 1999).

Chapter Seven

Multitasking and livelihood diversification

Studies of rural people living off the land have stressed the impact of non-farm employment as offering alternative livelihood to farming and anchoring the development of rural labour markets. Many studies with a rural development focus, however, have tended to place emphasis on the manner in which income from off-farm employment is allocated and distributed and the consequences on rural poverty or household welfare. Yet, although the term non-farm seems self-explanatory, there appears to be a lack of consensus on the way it is to be defined and used. Hence, the first part of this chapter will attempt to isolate notable arguments. Following immediately will be a review of factors contributing to growth and nurturing of non-farm activities. Suffice to state that actual outcomes vary in form and intensity owing to variations in specific enabling and disenabling conditions. The specific conditions may relate to particular social, cultural, economic, and spatial-ecological conditions. The non-farm sector generates earnings and remittances that alter the livelihood options open to individuals and households, how they negotiate livelihood uncertainty and contest underdevelopment perceived over a long period of time.

Multitasking as a norm

Quite often rural households are inaccurately classified as agricultural as if rural livelihoods and generally rural economies depend solely on production, consumption and distribution and exchange of farm products. Such a representation underplays the multi-activity nature of rural dwellers and households. Coincidentally, rural poverty and rural livelihood

135

insecurity are attributed to and explained erroneously in terms of the failure of agriculture to offer adequate sustenance, both in terms of food security and steady flows of cash income. Rather, since the late 1980s, studies on rural livelihood portfolios in many developing world have sufficiently demonstrated that households are rarely dependent on just one source of food or income, let alone solely on farming (Schejtman 1999; de Haan 2010). In most situations households rely on a combination of material resources such as farming, wages, and remittances, gifts from neighbours and relations and old age pension for retired civil servants and return urban immigrants (Zoomers 1999; Manona 2001; Araujo 2003).

In Malawi, studies on rural enterprises have shown clearly that rural livelihood strategies are becoming more diversified, with relatively more households engaged in agricultural labour off the family farm and operating micro-enterprises as illustrated in studies carried out at different times across a number of districts in central and southern Malawi (Hirschmann and Vaughan 1983 for Zomba; Mandala 1984 for the Lower Shire; Tellegen 1997 for Mchinji and Salima; Minde and Nakhumwa 1998 on cross-border trade; Englund 1999 for Dedza; Orr and Orr 2002 for Southern Malawi; Jimu 2011, 2012 for peri-urban Blantyre). It is apparent that rural livelihood security, let alone sustainable rural development, cannot be attained by a wholesale focus on agriculture to the neglect of alternative and complementary livelihood strategies. These alternatives are referred to as non-agricultural activities (NAA), non-farm economy, and non-agricultural rural economy (NARE). Household livelihood diversification is therefore a norm.

Rural livelihood diversification is equated to involvement in various non-agricultural activities, including non-farm activities carried out both in rural and urban areas. Migration as a livelihood strategy is an alternative strategy to non-agricultural activity in the broad sense. Chambers and Conway's (1992) defined livelihoods as comprising of activities, capabilities, and assets, while Scoones (2009) argued that livelihoods is a mobile and flexible concept. In Scoones' view, the concept 'livelihood' can be attached to other concepts to construct fields of development research and practice, for instance, locales (rural or urban livelihoods), occupations (farming, pastoral or fishing livelihoods), social difference (gendered or age-defined livelihoods), directions (livelihood pathways or trajectories), and dynamic patterns (sustainable or resilient livelihoods). Migration could support pursuit of both farm or agricultural and non-farm or non-agricultural livelihoods.

Definitions and implications

Throughout southern Africa many smallholder farm families are often not able to meet food and non-food needs solely from their own agricultural production. Non-agricultural activities take place both on the farm and off the farm and some are engaged in seasonal migrations to other rural and urban destinations where conditions are relatively better. That is, livelihood portfolios are constructed and negotiated around a triune of agriculture, non-farm activities and migration (Brycesson 1999).

By definition the rural non-farm economy comprises of income generating opportunities other than agriculture and gardening. Ellis (1997) summarized non-farm activity as non-agricultural in nature; while non-agricultural activities are any work that does not directly involve plant or animal husbandry. The Centre for Policy Dialogue (CPD) of Bangladesh states that the non-farm sector encompasses all non-crop activities in rural, semi-urban and peri-urban areas which may be sub-divided into two categories of farm-oriented non-farm activities linked to crop and non-crop enterprises and other activities such as trade, shop-keeping, construction, manufacturing, transport, and retail work (Centre for Policy Dialogue 2004). Waged labour or self-employment in small firms and petty crafts and sub-contracting for large manufacturing companies are some variants. The terms 'off-farm', 'non-farm', 'nonagricultural' and 'nontraditional' are in turn used to qualify the nature of the product, organization and the types of factors used in the production process. However, where the phrases 'rural geographic' or 'rural spatial location' is added, for example rural manufacturing as opposed to urban agriculture, sectoral inconsistencies are implied. Activities that are not confined to rural areas might be left out where a rural focus is overemphasized. It is also possible to exclude activities falling outside of agriculture such as forestry and fisheries when in fact they would include trade and processing of agricultural products taking place within rural geographic areas. To overcome this challenge the rural non-farm economy should be conceptualized simply as either waged or self-employed activities other than farming (Davis and Bezemer 2004). The pertinent issue becomes how are households intentionally diversifying into non-agricultural activities and perhaps pursuing more than one activity simultaneously or at different points throughout the year.

Diversification implies existence of a range of activities, investment strategies and reproductive choices. Chambers and Conway (1992) placed emphasis on the capabilities, assets (including both social and material resources) and activities. The reality is that livelihoods in many rural areas of the world involve complex and dynamic decision making processes. The complex and dynamic nature of livelihoods was recognized quite earlier, for example, by Wallman (1984) cited in Appendini (2001), Hussein and Nelson (1998), Bebbington (1999) and Francis and Murry (2002). From Wallman (1984) it appears that:

> Livelihood is never just a matter of finding or making shelter, transacting money, getting food to put on the family table or to exchange on the market place. It is equally a matter of ownership and circulation of information, the management of skills and relationships and the affirmation of personal significance and group identity. The tasks of meeting obligations, of security, identity and status, and organizing time are as crucial to livelihood as bread and shelter (Appendini 2001:25).

Bebbington (1999:2022), on the other hand, summarized a livelihood as involving assets, capabilities and agency in the following words:

'A person's assets, such as land, are not merely means with which he or she makes a living: they also give meaning to that person's world. Assets are not simply resources that people use in building livelihoods: they are assets that give them the capability to be and to act. Assets should not be understood only as things that allow survival, adaptation and poverty eradication: they are also the basis of agents' power to act and to reproduce, challenge or change the rules that govern the control, use and transformation of resources.'

The agentive role of individuals is brought to the fore in Hussein and Nelson (1998). For them livelihood diversification implies attempts by individuals and households to find new ways to earn a living, including raising incomes and reducing environmental risk. However, in situations where livelihoods have been solely agricultural in nature, diversification connotes transformation of the economy into new mainly non-agricultural sectors. It is for this reason that Ellis (1977) defined diversification as the process by which rural families construct a diverse portfolio of activities and social support capabilities. Diversification is further described as a phenomenon by which small farm households take up non-farm activities or rely on non-farm income transfers (Ellis 2005).

The most striking feature about diversified rural livelihoods is not the presence of urban and non-agricultural components but the continued persistence of part-time agriculture. As Ellis (2005) also observed this situation suggests that farming is for one reason or another unable to satisfy the basic requirements. Often livelihood strategies are in a state of flux as people adapt to evolving threats and opportunities, changing livelihood objectives or as their own capabilities change. It is also possible along the same vein for livelihood diversification to emerge not always as an outcome of some conscious effort. This is true as a study of non-farm economy in Uganda revealed that the rural populations do not always make conscious decision to avoid or supplement their farming activities in order to engage specifically in non- farm activities, rather non- farm activities are a part of a range of possible livelihood options (Cannon and Smith 2002). Alternative livelihood activities are always carried out during the off-season as part of the farming cycle while in other cases non-farm activities involve assets that are liquidated to overcome livelihood shocks. Therefore non-farm activities are not something that is distinct and desirable because they substitute farm or agricultural activities, but these activities are better understood as forming part of a range of livelihood opportunities; being both flexible, negotiable and interchangeable.

A number of equally important studies have pursued the agenda of how livelihoods can cope with and recover from stresses and shocks, and the resilience required. Among them are de Haan and Zoomers (2003) whose major contribution to the debate is the recognition that stresses and shocks that affect livelihoods result from interactions between global forces and local contexts. These may include fluctuations in resources, seasonal variations, economic drivers (world markets, unaffordable credit) and policy drivers (misguided government programs) (Marschkei and Berkes 2006). Related to the above are studies that have emphasized the building up of resilience and sustainability.

Drawing on Scoones (1998) sustainable livelihoods could be summarized as:

> 'Given a particular *context* (of policy setting, politics, history, agro ecology and socio-economic conditions), what combination of *livelihood resources* (different types of 'capital') result in the ability to follow what combination of *livelihood strategies* (agricultural intensification/extensification, livelihood diversification and migration) with what *outcomes?* Of particular interest in this framework are the *institutional processes* (embedded in a matrix of formal and informal institutions and organizations) which mediate the ability to carry out such strategies and achieve (or not) such outcomes.'

The challenge has been 'definitions of sustainable livelihoods are often unclear, inconsistent and relatively narrow. Without clarification, there is a risk of simply adding to a conceptual muddle...'[1]

Rural livelihood strategies are shaped by a wide range of factors and motivations. With reference to studies in the Andean region Valdivia and Quiroz (2001) argued that climate is perhaps the most important natural factor affecting production and consumption decisions. Other significant factors include: access and control of human, natural, productive, cultural and social capital; markets; institutions; and the political environment. Livelihood strategies are further, influenced by linkages in and outside agriculture, life cycle, education level and the number of family members. The degree of diversification of household portfolio is also determined by the household's and individual's objectives, risk management practices, and strategies available for coping with shocks. It follows that in areas of greater risk household strategies are expected to be more diversified so as to minimize possible shocks from negative climatic events, especially when loss-management strategies are limited (Valdivia and Quiroz 2001). Diversification in agriculture and in nonagricultural activities may take place as a result of accumulation of capital and assets. As families become old and resources are bequeathed, livelihoods become less diversified once again. The tangible resources - natural, human, cultural, social and productive, and the intangibles (claims and access) impact on the ability to negotiate combinations of livelihood activities.

Hussein and Nelson (1998) have demonstrated the significance of livelihood diversification by drawing examples on the level of diversification in Burkina Faso. Livelihood diversification allows surpluses to be generated that can then be invested in a variety of other activities. Across West Africa income diversification is associated with more stable incomes and improved consumption patterns. However, as Hussein and Nelson also showed, the possibility that livelihood diversification leads to income, which is used for investment, is generally dependent on initial wealth. Berry (1989) noted earlier that poor producers are unlikely to be able to use income from livelihood diversification for agricultural intensification, but rather use it to support consumption and essential current expenses that support survival rather than accumulation. As Dercon and Krishnan (1996) have also shown for rural Tanzania and Ethiopia different income portfolios held by households cannot be explained by their behaviour towards risk. Instead, the ability of households to adopt more profitable diversification strategies depends on access to the means required to pursue those activities such as skills, location, livestock ownership, access to capital and credit.

It is almost impossible to generalize factors that lead to livelihood diversification let alone the degree of involvement in various non-farm activities. Factors motivating diversification into the non-farm economy can however be better understood by appreciating existence of two categories of activities within the non-farm sector: some that are productive and others that have low productivity (Araujo 2003). The latter contribute to the incomes of the poor, but do not allow for social and economic mobility. Such activities are residual occupations people are driven into and they reflect growing desperation. The de-agrarianization and rural employment (DARE) survey reported that rural women in Tanzania often referred to income-earning roles as having been thrust upon them by worsening economic circumstances (Bryceson 1999). Manona (2001) commenting on rural enterprises in southern Africa noted that in most cases non-farm activities appear to be a last resort than an attractive alternative livelihood. Often people involved in them earn very little for their effort and what they earn is often irregular. Considering that most non-farm activities yield very low returns, diversification of rural livelihood strategies may thus contribute less to positive dynamic- economic growth and shift in employment from agriculture to industry and to services (Schejtman 1999). Yet, such activities are important from a social welfare perspective. The income from such activities contribute to the reduction of aggregate income inequality, seasonal or long-term unemployment, and also offer some form of low level economic security, the size and relevance of non-farm economy notwithstanding.

The size of the rural non-farm economy has been a matter of speculation. First and foremost there is lack of consensus on its character and there are no reliable statistics and on the actual contribution that such activities make to rural economies. World Bank estimates on rural non-farm activities for close to a decade ago showed that such activities contribute between 40 and 50% of total rural household incomes in El Salvador, Ecuador and Mexico; on average between 30 and 50% in sub-Saharan Africa; and up to 80% in South Africa (Araujo 2003). The same report further noted that in the 1990s non-farm incomes in rural India represented 34% of total household incomes. An earlier report suggested that on average non-farm activities provide 20 to 45% of full-time employment and 30 to 50% of rural household incomes in Africa (Liedholm et al. 1994). As Ellis (1998) also noted the proportion varies widely between, for example, landless households and those with access to land for farming.

A more qualitative account of the rural non-farm activities in Bangladesh noted that rural non-farm activities are quite diverse engaging both skilled and unskilled labour and both male and female, and yet most segments are residual in nature (Center for Policy Dialogue 2004). There is strong evidence that participation in rural non-farm activities is skewed in favour of men. For instance, in rural areas of Mali 84% of

145

participants in the rural non-farm economy in the 1990s were often men (Hussein and Nelson (1998:9).

Non-farm economy and poverty

Diversification into the rural non-farm activities involves allocation of household productive assets among different income generating activities. The viability of rural non-farm activities rests in understanding that they constitute alternative sources of livelihood, alternative means to economic empowerment, alternative poverty reduction strategies, alternative means to rural development and capacity to cope with climatic risk and to maximize use of resources. Schejtman summarized the potential effects of the rural non-farm economy in the following words:

> Non-agricultural activities play an important and growing role in absorbing the rural labour force; it is a means of relieving poverty that agriculture alone cannot offer, it makes it possible to stabilize income, making up for the seasonal nature of agricultural production and employment; and it makes it possible to diversify sources of income, thus reducing the effects of the risks which are inherent in agriculture' (Schejtman 1999:26)

It appears therefore that the rural non-farm economy may absorb rural surplus labour, help farm based households spread risks, offer more remunerative activities to supplement or replace agriculture, provide a means for the rural people to cope or survive when farming fails, exploit rural comparative advantages, foster rural growth and improve the overall quality of life (Davis and Bezemer 2004). These contributions are also significant for food security, poverty alleviation and farm sector competitiveness. However, there is need to understand existence of two subcategories of livelihood diversification: positive diversification and negative diversification. On one hand, positive diversification would involve greater productivity while negative diversification would involve lower productivity. Sectors associated with positive forms of diversification are likely to include those linked to urban markets and rural 'exports' or growth engines, while negative diversification is linked to coping strategies.

It has been shown that rural non-farm enterprises adapt to market signals, and for this reason promise to absorb increasing proportion of the rural labour force (Murty 2005 writing on rural non-agricultural employment in India). In the process rural non-farm enterprises also moderate the socially and economically harmful effects of rural-urban migration (Kabra 2005: 35). Further, some activities have greater capacity to stimulate and get stimulated by the growth of the agricultural sector, hence triggering a virtuous cycle of growth and development, reducing the distress sale of agricultural produce, acting as a hedge against crop failure, as an instrument for income redistribution, and as a safety-net to prevent the poor from falling even further into poverty (Murty 2005 for India; Escobar 2001 for Peru; Reardon et al. 2001 broadly for Latin America).

Non-agricultural employment in Malawi

Taking a relatively long timeframe, livelihood diversification and more specifically non-agricultural activities are not a new phenomenon as has otherwise been suggested in some recent studies. Subsequent sections will examine the situation as it were from the colonial into the post-colonial era. This long term perspective will illuminate issues and challenges that have often eluded policy makers and development agencies.

To begin with agriculture and long distance trade existed before establishment of colonial rule in the last decade of the 19th Century even as it is difficult to pin point with certainty the genesis of long distance exchange economy. Per Lindskog observed that pre-colonial economic activities were far more varied and complex than supposed by many administrators during the colonial period (Lindskog 1982). The misleading impression created then was that economies of pre-colonial period Malawi were mainly subsistence, only transformed into market economies during the colonial period. Historical studies on pre-colonial trade (Alpers (1975), Bhila (1975) and Phiri (1976) cited in Lindskog 1982), however, illustrate complex traditional exchange economies. In fact it has been suggested that iron, salt, locally made cotton clothes, livestock among others were exchanged on local and regional scales. The boom in inter-regional trade in slaves and ivory in the 19th century actually increased exploitation of other resources, including agricultural ones. Most exchange during the pre-colonial period was organized along more informal lines such that colonial control simply reoriented those trade patterns by the institutionalization of the marketplace exchange. New goods and services and government-enforced economic or labour demand led to a situation where needs could only be met by participation in the cash-based market economy through the sale of labour or agricultural produce.

While many natives relied on subsistence or semi-subsistence cultivation as is the case to date, some who were literate were employed as clerks by European and Indian owned businesses (Mitchell 1968). Many more natives worked as unskilled labourers and personal servants. Consolidation of colonial rule before and after the World War I created new opportunities for non-farm work, though such opportunities were not always driven by choice. For instance, adult male natives were required to perform forced labour for twenty four days in a year in construction or maintenance work of public nature for the benefit of the area they belonged to. Natives, mostly males, were also liable to compulsory paid labour for government transport and for the construction of public buildings, railways, telephone lines, sanitary works (District Administration (Native) Ordinance 1924). Non-agricultural activities into which natives could enter voluntarily were apparently few and in some districts virtually almost absent. Hence, the consolidation of colonial rule facilitated internal migration, mainly to the Shire Highlands in southern Malawi.

The Shire Highlands is home to the following ethnic groups: Mang'anja (closely related to Nyanja of the Lake Malawi area and the Chewa of central Malawi), the Yao and the Lomwe listed by order of settlement. Today, the Yao and the Lomwe stand out as the most predominant groups in the area and as such the following analysis will focus on these two groups. Mitchell writes that traditionally men in Yao villages were involved in trading and slave raiding expeditions, but during her fieldwork in the 1940s some men were absent as soldiers, and some had migrated to Zimbabwe (then Southern Rhodesia) or South Africa (then Union of South Africa). An economic survey in the Domasi area of Zomba district in 1949[2] found that about 30% of able-bodied men were quite often absent from home, either as labour migrants, or in employment or on trade errands within the country (Hirschmann and Vaughan 1983). These migrants were providing or supporting their families and households, despite that the village communities were then capable of self-supporting mainly from subsistence food production and cash crops (Mitchell 1968).

Colonial rule accelerated migratory patterns and created new ones. Initially, most migrant labourers were seasonal and temporary. In the 1920s it was estimated that thirty thousand Malawians were working outside Malawi during each year (Buell 1965). Some estimates show that in the 1930s half of the able bodied men in the northern part of Malawi were often absent from their home as migrant labourers in the southern part or outside Malawi. Many migrated because of the prospects of earning money for food, clothing, shelter, and money for bride price, and for buying bicycles, but most importantly money for paying taxes following the imposition of hut and poll taxes. These taxes were introduced to cover administrative costs (Hull 1980).

As the years passed, many rural households began to get involved in some trading, especially of various agricultural products. Then, as now, any farm produce could be sold for cash, implying that no crop was entirely a subsistence crop.

Notably much of the cash income realized from the sale of agricultural produce was often used for the purchase of salt from Indian traders or African canteen holders (Mitchell 1968). The main crops frequently sold included maize, sorghum and cassava. These were supplemented by finger millet, sweet potatoes, ground nuts, legumes, and rice. Fruits, both wild and cultivated, mainly mangoes, bananas, pawpaw, oranges and lemons were also widely available for food and for cash income. In Mitchell's study, rice was produced and traded particularly in villages near Lake Chirwa in present day districts of Zomba and Machinga. The main market for crops happened to be produce markets run by the Agricultural Department, although all the crops were also sold along roads and at government controlled produce markets. Earliest forms of government controlled pricing of farm produce were applied to tobacco, cotton and maize. For instance, the price of 'surplus' maize sold in government produce markets was controlled, though there was no similar control over the sale of maize between Africans (Mitchell 1968). A further dimension observed by Mitchell in the 1940s, and also by Hirschmann and Vaughan (1983) in the late 1970s in Zomba was that women earned cash by selling flour and brewing beer. The colonial government attempted to regulate beer brewing and selling through club houses, ostensibly to control drunkenness (Mitchell 1968).

The existence of some form of petty trading is reflected in historical accounts that suggest that throughout much of Africa petty trading in locally manufactured goods such as cloth, blankets, and woodcarvings garden crops, and livestock became an important activity as early as the 1920s (Hull 1980).

The challenge was that natives often failed to make progress in business because of various challenges, most of which underlie current lukewarm participation in business enterprises. One of the challenges rooted in the nature of extended family networks was overspending of profits on supporting close kin and non-filial relations. The other challenge is that trading passed from European to Asian traders. Overtime, good knowledge of bookkeeping, efficiency at ploughing back or reinvesting profits into stock, well established sources of goods overseas and easy access to credit from local banks gave Asian traders competitive edge over African merchants (Hull 1980). Slow development of transport and communications had its own share of limiting native enterprises. In the case of Malawi, some Yao, who were initially caravan traders tried cotton production but gave up due to high transport cost (McCraken 1986). McCraken further suggests that later the Yao turned to wage labour as unskilled porters, then as policemen and soldiers with the King's African Rifles, providing close to half of Nyasaland's battalions. By 1938, the once prosperous area of Makanjira on the southern-eastern side of Lake Malawi could no longer feed itself and was designated a 'distressed area'. As McCraken further argued this was a result of colonial policy of undermining regimes which had relied on raiding, tribute and cattle accumulation.

Among other ethnic groups, the Lomwe of the Shire Highlands, the heartland of colonial rule, started with *thangata* system, which offered some subsistence compared to the harsh conditions in neighbouring Mozambique (then Portuguese East Africa). These early experiences eventually stimulated the export of labour through the Witwatersrand Native Labour

Association (WNLA) (McCraken 1986). Migration, whether internal or external, implied long periods of physical separation of household family members. As shown by Mitchell (1968) having been practiced for a long period of time, it became a norm for males to enter into labour migration. In the early years women stayed back. Households survived largely on subsistence food production and cash remittances from male migrants.

The connection between smallholder agriculture and labour migration has been strong for livelihood security as shown in the study by Mandala (1984), which elaborates on the links between agricultural and non-agricultural economies in the colonial era, more especially in the Shire valley. Initially, in the lower Shire Valley communities started producing and trading sesame seed. While villages in the northern part of the Shire, both men and women, sold their seed to local traders, in the southern part the men alone took their produce to the Zambezian markets by canoe. Male domination of the non-agricultural economy eventually declined in the face of increasing competition from imports and as the economies became more exclusively centred on agricultural household-based production. This tendency was enhanced by colonial intervention, in particular, by the introduction and adoption of cotton as a cash crop in the first decade of the 20th century. When cotton production collapsed, rich smallholder farmers responded and were successful at diversifying and investing in grain mills, canteens, cattle and fishing nets. Notably, many people living along the Shire River took on fishing on a serious note. However, fishing became an important activity following the growth of Blantyre and Limbe as important urban centres.

153

These dimensions signal cumulative and differential opportunities over time and the transformative effects of urbanization on rural livelihoods in the early years of colonial rule in Malawi. The cumulative effects are further manifest in the rise of livestock production as an important aspect of rural life in the Shire valley both during colonial and post-colonial times. For the Lower Shire Valley, before the 20th century there were no African-owned cattle, but the number of cattle has since risen remarkably from just 300 heard by 1935 to 5,000 by 1955 and to over 100,000 in 1980 (Mandala, 1984). From the meagre beginnings the Shire Valley is today the main supplier of meat to Blantyre city's 600,000 plus population.

In the post-independence era, successive governments have strongly promoted, even if only at rhetorical level, the agro-bias approach to rural livelihoods. A study completed over eight years ago showed that 27% of household heads are engaged in more than one activity, 32% of farm households have two sources of income, and 42% have three or more sources of income (World Bank 2006). An earlier report titled *A Relative Profile of Poverty 1998* (Government of Malawi 2001) showed that the wealthy are more likely to be formally employed than are the less wealthy, while heads of households in the poorest households are more likely than other heads of household to be home workers. Another notable observation is that while poorer individuals tend to be self-employed in non-farm businesses related to forestry, fishing, and mining, individuals from wealthier households are more likely to be employed by government or private businesses. One of the factors contributing to self-employment among the poor is various attempts by the government to promote rural

154

entrepreneurial culture. One of early attempts was the 1978 Business Licensing Act which introduced provisions prohibiting all Asians from carrying out trading activities in places other than urban centres, ostensibly to protect native traders from competition.[3] Instead and on a negative note, the impact has been decay of physical infrastructure at affected rural market centres countrywide, and in some cases Malawian traders have abandon such centres leading to rural retail blight.

The reasons for the multiplicity of livelihoods are varied as will be shown by the review of studies carried out since the late 1970s, for example, by Hirschmann and Vaughan (1983), Tellegen (1997), the Livelihoods and Diversification Directions Explored by Research (LADDER) project of the University of East Anglia and my own fieldwork in peri-urban Blantyre. These studies show, as de Haan (2010) writes on perspectives on African studies and livelihoods that the multiplicity of economic activities reflects the creativity of actors and their ability to combine diverging and often widely dispersed resources into a livelihood. While opportunities for off-farm employment are limited, or few poor households are often involved in trade, or have a shop, those with skills work as artisans, for example, as carpenters or tinsmiths. Other households earn money from charcoal making, cutting thatching grass, or fishing, while women earn cash from brewing beer and food vending. For poorer households, the main and often the only source of non-farm income represented in all the studies cited above is *ganyu* (piece work).

Hirschmann and Vaughan studied 54 villages in Zomba district, within a radius of 20 miles of the Zomba municipality. Zomba was Malawi's capital up to 1975. They conducted the study between April and June 1981. These months coincide with the main harvest of rain fed crops, including maize. Their study showed that by the end of the 1970s rural households had reached a critical point characterized by low land holdings. Landholdings were already too small that intensification of labour and application of fertilizer could hardly lead to increased output and food and income security. As a consequence households were engaged in and also depended on various forms of non-agricultural income. Among men, non-agricultural income sources included permanent employment in government departments, as domestic servants, and as migrant labour outside Malawi, or non-permanent employment in trades and agricultural labour. Trading of *dimba* crops and grain, beer brewing and *ganyu* were among the important sources of income among women. As Hirschmann and Vaughan (1983) noted, a majority of women, 80% of the total sampled, earned cash income primarily from selling own agricultural produce. Apparently, households sold food even where they had low stocks that could not satisfy domestic requirements. Some people accepted off-farm income as central to their survival, but access to land and well paid employment or profitable trade were ranked highly and so were considered significant in explaining long term economic differentiation.

The study by Tellegen (1997), which was in essence a longitudinal study of rural enterprises in 1983 and 1993 in Mchinji and Salima districts in central Malawi, delves into the evolving structure of rural livelihoods in districts with a large number of households engaged in smallholder commercial production of tobacco. Tellegen observed that the proportion of total household income derived from non-agricultural sources was 21% among the poorest, 60% in the second highest income group, and 55% in the wealthiest group. In the wealthiest group, agriculture happened to the most important household income source, yet high-income farming heads of households earned more income from non-agricultural activities compared to other households. Such households earned 2.5 times more than middle income household heads, and 10 times more than lower-income household heads. Middle and low-income groups, who were not able to pursue the highest non-agricultural income-earning activities, were nonetheless fundamentally dependent on non-agricultural sources for their livelihood. The other important observation was that very few people actually specialize in non-agricultural activities. More than 90% combined non-agricultural activities with farming, regardless of whether they were subsistence or commercial farmers. A smaller group of about 18% was involved in farming only. For more than 70% of the households that were involved in self-employment outside the agricultural sector, income from self-employment was observed to be higher than income from farming. Only 4% of the households specialized in non-agricultural activities, and the few in this category were in the richest strata of the population. Only 25% of the households were involved in wage labour. Wages or income were however generally higher than farming incomes, but lower than those from non-agricultural activities. As a result, only 2% of the households specialized in wage labour. Tellegen further shows that while in many cases the motive behind diversification appears to spread risks in an uncertain economic environment, some diversified because it was virtually impossible to expand existing businesses due to low levels of demand. There were others who kept businesses small to avoid the image of being 'rich' entrepreneur. In doing so they also avoided attracting too many relatives requesting for assistance. Finally, while the number of rural households that can benefit from non-agricultural activity is limited by high levels of start-up capital that preclude farmers of more modest means, investment in non-agricultural activity provided the road to rural wealth.

Turning to the Livelihoods and Diversification Directions Explored by Research (LADDER) funded by the Department for International Development (DFID), the core focus was to explore alternative routes by which the rural poor can come out of poverty. Of the 37 village reports produced from studies in Kenya, Malawi, Tanzania and Uganda, eight focused on livelihoods in Malawian villages, of which six were drawn from Dedza district in central Malawi and 2 from Zomba district in southern Malawi. Two study reports of Katanda Village in Zomba and Lumwira Village in Dedza will be appraised here. Katanda village is located in Zomba district, not too far from the site of an earlier study by Hirschmann and Vaughan (1983). Due to diminishing returns from agricultural activities many poor households were engaged in *ganyu*, while others were involved in petty trading, including the selling of bananas, sugarcane, *kalingonda* (a kind of beans that is toxic if not prepared well), fishing floats, and fuel wood. These activities are on the increase and are increasingly being pursued because they provide opportunity to combat food insecurity.[4] Migration to other districts to work as estate tenants or domestic servants, servicing bicycles for fish traders, operating tea rooms, making bricks, collecting and selling thatch for roofing houses were reported. In the case of Lumwira Village in Dedza, villagers grow both food and cash crops. Cash crops include groundnuts, soya beans, peas and beans, while maize, cassava and sweet potatoes are grown for food. Alternative activities include beer brewing, selling bananas and Irish potatoes, carpentry work and *ganyu*. Most of the non-agricultural activities were reported to be poorly developed because of lack of capital and lack of entrepreneurial development and management skills. Coping and adaptive livelihood strategies included *Msuma* also known as *ganyu*; migrating to the cities in search of low paid jobs; and selling mice and firewood along the major road. A further important activity was hiring out farm carts, mostly used to transport firewood and farm produce.[5] Livestock kept in the village included cattle, goats, pigs and chickens. While cattle were kept by 'well-to-do' households only, most households had goats, pigs, and chickens. Livestock contributed to household incomes in meaningful ways. The challenge was that the number of livestock was declining as a result of theft and diseases.

Similar aspects emerged in my recent study on peri-urban land transactions in Blantyre (Jimu 2011, 2012). Besides small-scale farming, many peri-urban villagers are engaged in diverse economic activities, including hiring out labour. Off-farm activities are largely confined to seasonal labour, food vending and marketing of farm produce. Vending as an occupation is quite diverse. Small girls and boys and the elderly sell flitters, sugarcane, sweet potatoes, tomatoes, maize flour, groundnuts and rape. The boom in vending of this form is linked to the rise in per-urban population thanks to rising peri-urban land transactions described in the previous chapter. Vending entails different payment practices, including payment in cash or on credit. Trading of this type is also common in the cities where traders move from house to house and sometimes from one office to another with items such as raw and prepared food, livestock (chickens, pigeons, guinea fowls, ducks and goats), and second hand (used) clothes. Other forms of activity include barber shops, tea rooms and mini grocery stores (offering candles, salt, sugar, soap, matches, school and stationery supplies etc.). Roadside vending is important for women and the merchandise traded include second hand clothes and maize and maize husks (*madeya*) used in distilling spirit (*kachasu*) and also as feed for chickens, cattle and pigs. Roadside vending extends to workshops where various items are fabricated. These workshops include metal products fabricators, carpentry workshops and bicycle repair shops. Further, there is substantial trading in charcoal, a phenomenon associated with deforestation in the areas where it is produced (Blantyre District Assembly 2007).

Other important non-agricultural activities include the triad of sand mining, brick making and artisan quarrying. The mining of sand takes place mostly in the rainy season when the streams are flooded with water. The filling up of streams with water is accompanied by deposition of loads of sand washed from the deforested catchment areas. Both men and women are engaged in sand mining. Sand mining involves dredging the river bed to take out the sand. Where the work is done by married couples the role played by women is often to transfer the sand from the river bank to the place where it is loaded into lorries. The boom in the construction industry means that the demand for sand is usually high. Brick making is an old industry facing ups and downs due to the boom in the construction of houses and the depletion of wood used in the curing of bricks. Depletion of wood means that fewer people are now involved in brick making than before and in some cases some people go into it even when they are not certain about how to source the required fuel wood. Above all waged labour (ganyu) has become for many peri-urban villages, especially among young men, a major source of income.

Waged labour especially understood as work off one's own farm regardless whether the work is farm or non-farm related, represents a special form of non-agricultural activity. Based on fieldwork in Dedza, Englund (1999) showed that *ganyu* is the most common way of recruiting agricultural labour from outside the household. The use of cash in *Ganyu* does not mean that these labour arrangements are devoid of social obligations. Englund showed that the practice of labour pulling or sharing (work parties) is rare and wherever it occurs participation is rewarded with beer. Most often, *ganyu* is offered to kin, especially those from within the matrilineage, probably because of the matrilineal nature of the groups, which also defines access to productive assets in land. Englund and the LADDER studies mentioned already have shown how families living closer to the border with Mozambique and Zambia seek *Ganyu* work in these countries at peak times of planting and weeding or in land preparation for winter cropping in wetland. This practice implies how unbounded diversified livelihoods are by state boundaries. Ethnic and familial and non-familial ties transcend state or territorial boundaries.

Further examples of the significance of *ganyu* in cross border communities are provided for communities living in south east Malawi. There is also growing short term (one day to a few weeks) cross-border migration between Malawi and Mozambican among smallholder farmers. For instance, in some border villages in Mulanje district, up to 75% of the households have someone doing ganyu in Mozambique. Ganyu provides an important source of food, although such work also conflict with work needed to be done on one's own farm. The significance of this trend could also be felt in the Mozambique side where it is felt to be an important aspect for intensification of smallholders, who with access to plenty of land often find labour shortage to be a main constraint to increasing production (see Whiteside 1998). Ganyu in this part of Malawi is important considering that for some villagers the key source of food is informal food imports from Mozambique. Some households rely on such food imports for between four and nine months each year. The slightly better off earn much of their living from buying food, mainly maize, in Mozambique and selling it either in their own community or in local markets from where it is generally sold to Blantyre (Whiteside 1998).

That ganyu is associated with vulnerability is further reported in the 2007 vulnerability assessment by USAID in the following terms:

'Most of the poor households in the country depend on providing agricultural casual labour (*ganyu*) to obtain incomes to buy food when their own produced food stocks run out. In times of food shortage, the number of people looking for *ganyu* increases and the wage rate falls significantly as *ganyu* seekers are willing to accept almost any wage rate just to make it through. Conversely, in a good year, the number of *ganyu* seekers declines, even as agricultural activities such as land preparation have started in many parts of the country. The wage rates are in some areas reportedly at around MK1,500 per acre from about MK600 per acre during the same time last season, an increase of over 50%, reflecting the current scarcity of available labour, which in some areas is difficult to find.'[6]

However, the practice of *ganyu* has often been misrepresented. For instance, Kulemeka (2000) pointed out that the notion that *ganyu* is the principal coping strategy in Malawi embodies a view of the typical Malawian household as a rural smallholder family. In that way, urban households, tenants on estates and other minority groups are not treated as distinct categories with their own set of. Further, he points that differences in coping within households – specifically, between the coping behaviours of men and women, or between male – and female-headed households - are sometimes underrepresented in discussions of how 'Malawian households' cope with drought or restricted access to agricultural inputs. The other dimension missed in many analysis of *ganyu* is the view that it entails work done outside the household, but reality is that age mediates the practice such that young children are mobilized to work on their own family farm sometimes on *ganyu* terms.[7]

Recently, *ganyu* has been institutionalized by the state and the development partners in the name of public works programme (PWPs). The national public works programme was first implemented in July 1995 on a pilot basis under the Malawi Social Action Fund (MASAF), and later in July 1996 as a national intervention programme (Chirwa 2007). It will be noted that many institutions have been implementing PWPs, including: the Government of Malawi/European Union, CARE International, World Vision International, Catholic Relief Services (CRS), Malawi Red Cross, Save the Children – UK, the Salvation Army, Emmanuel International, Save the Children – US, and Africare (see Chirwa 2007). PWP is considered one of the important tools of helping the most vulnerable groups. MASAF implemented various public works programmes with different design features, including the Improved Livelihoods through Public Works Programme (ILTPWP) in 2003, the Emergency Drought Recovery Programme (EDRP-PWP) between 2002 and 2004 and the Public Works Programme-Conditional Cash Transfer (PWP-CCT) in 2005 (Chirwa 2007). PWP activities have also been linked to the fertilizer input subsidy programme (FISP).

By design, PWP are characterized by use of a minimum wage as a self-targeting mechanism, work norms based on task rates, shorter duration employment reaching, and local participation and collaboration of various institutions (Chirwa 2007). Like with TIP and FISP the challenge has been how to target the poor in a country where the majority are quite poor. Devereux et al. (2006) cited in Chirwa (2007) noted the importance of having targeted intervention that aims to protect the vulnerable and promote the livelihoods of the poor, but argued that such targeting requires accurate identification of those who need different types of assistance, to minimize both inclusion and exclusion errors. Lack of or imperfect information on degrees of poverty makes targeting criteria for public works employment problematic as it has been for farm input subsidy arrangements.

For the peri-urban villagers in Blantyre the significance of the practice of ganyu is now linked closely with the practice of selling of land, as it means having to learn to live with less and sometimes without land. Loss is literary manifest where the villagers cannot collect wood for fuel, grass for thatching and loss of the right of passage after land providing these resources has been sold. Peri-urban land transactions are eventually transforming smallholder farmers into landless *ganyu* seekers. Some young people often talk about *ganyu* with a sense of pride and optimism. Often they highlight how easy it is in the current set up to find piecework in comparison to the past few years. *Ganyu* offers a window for understanding how the peri-urban villagers attempt to make sense and also adapt to changing configuration of livelihood options (Jimu 2011, 2012).

The dynamics of ganyu in peri-urban Blantyre reflect in part challenges of economic liberalization. That is, many farmers in peri-urban zones in Africa have had to make hard decisions, which include selling land, a trend few would have been prepared to contemplate some decades earlier. Experiences in peri-urban Blantyre show that there are many factors other than indirect effect of economic liberalizations. The wages from *ganyu* are sometimes unreasonably low relative to the rising cost of living. Some people do ganyu on the land that they sold away. When doing *ganyu* in such a situation the feeling is no longer that 'I am working on my garden' but doing *ganyu* on the boss's land. As Janine Ubink suggests, the sale of land automatically implies the loss of farmland for a local farmer, which often severely affects the person's livelihood. Such effects are difficult to cope with or turn around even if the sale of land provides good start-up capital for a new livelihood (Ubink (2008:279). Those who have some land have some flexibility. They can combine *ganyu* and some form of subsistence production of food. Hence, although many people accept *ganyu* as central to their livelihood access to land and paid employment or profitable trade are considered significant for any meaningful long term wellbeing.

Developmental potential of non-agricultural activities

The questions addressed in the following sections is whether and how the poor could actually benefit from non-agricultural activities. Wandschneider and Junior (2003) noted that direct participation by the poorest in rural non-farm economy seems rare. In fact the majority of beneficiaries in projects promoting non-farm activities tend to belong to the middle strata of rural communities. They argued that the poorest of the poor tend to lack the minimal asset base and risk-bearing capacity required for participation in more viable non-farm activities because they lack requisite capacity other than providing waged labour. It appears that the landless and marginal farming households, for instance, cannot participate and benefit adequately in many initiatives that work with farmers to add value to their agricultural production because most remunerative manufacturing and service activities have investment, working capital and skill requirements which are often beyond the capacity of the poor. They also noted that the more ambitious the marketing strategy, the greater the potential for financial gain but also the higher the risks incurred and the more stringent the entry barriers to the poor. However, they also noted that local development potential of non-farm activities is not limited by the lack of participation by the poorest of the poor since from a long term local development perspective, some non-farm activities can serve as local development engines due to their growth potential and the consumption and production linkages associated with them. Even where the poor are excluded from self-employment as entrepreneurs, they may benefit from improved local wage opportunities and availability of goods and services.

The challenges the poorest of the poor encounter are well illustrated by a comparative study of rural livelihood and poverty reduction strategies in four African countries of Kenya, Malawi, Tanzania and Uganda (Ellis and Freeman (2002). The study noted that access to non-farm activities makes households better off and differential access to such opportunities lead to significant differences in inter-household welfare, and sometimes such activities widen the income gap between households. They observed in the four countries that households with access to non-farm incomes were able to hire labour to undertake cultivation and to purchase farm inputs, while households without non-farm cash incomes hired out labour at times when they had to work in their own gardens. Hence, the agricultural production of the poor households remained stagnant or declined. They concluded that it follows that 'poor households tend to be net sellers rather than buyers of labour, they are seasonally food insecure in most years, and they engage in few or no non-farm activities' (Ellis and Freeman, (2002:9). The challenge is that the poor tend to be

167

involved in low return activities catering for saturated markets. The benefits are limited and crowd-out.

Within sub-Saharan Africa reliance on agriculture tends to diminish continuously as income level rises, that is, the more diverse the income portfolio the better-off is the rural household (Ellis, 1998). However, in the case of Nigeria, Mustapha (1999) as cited in Bryceson (1999) reported on the benefit of time series data for cocoa-producing area which showed a remarkable rise in household participation in non-farm activities from an average of 33% in the mid-1980s to 57% in 1997 at the time of the DARE survey. When broken down by income group, there were striking differences: the low-income group's participation increases dramatically from 35% to 80% while that of the upper income group declined from 33% to 25%. The middle income group jumped from 30 to 50% over the same period. It is evident therefore that while diversity of income sources is prevalent across different income classes, the nature of this diversification differs between better off and poorer households. In the case of Ethiopia Carswell (2002) noted that the single most important non-farm activity is trading, involving roughly 14% of adults. The next most important diversification activity is casual labour with 4% of adults involved. The better off tend to diversify in the form of non-farm business activities (trade, transport, shop keeping, brick making etc.) or salaried employment, while the poor tend to diversify in the form of casual wage work, especially on other farms, while remaining heavily reliant on subsistence crop production.

De-agrarianisation and re-agrarinisation

Agriculture and non-agricultural activities are not mutually exclusive but the actual relationship between the two is sometimes contested as it is not clear cut. In societies and countries where agriculture contributes a larger proportion to gross domestic income the pattern of rural non-agricultural activities is likely to closely mirror the overall performance of agriculture. Ellis (1999) noted that conventional wisdom shows that rising output and incomes in agriculture is a catalyst for diversification into non-agricultural activities. The argument is that agricultural growth, often associated with modernization of production does not only increase farmers' access to food and income, but it creates new employment opportunities in the farm and off-farm sectors. In this view modernization of agricultural sector could be one of the prime movers for emergence of non-agricultural and non-farm sectors. Modernization requires injection of significant amount of micro-credit and remittances, creation of markets and good prices, and government-led improvements in physical infrastructure (Centre for Policy Dialogue (Bangladesh) 2004:5) which provide conducive conditions for the growth of non-agricultural activities. Similar trends have been reported in Latin America where the growth of the rural non-agricultural activities in the 1990s highlighted the importance of modernization of agriculture and the integration between rural and urban labour markets (de Silva et al. 1999:14).

Other studies have shown that the growth of the non-agricultural sector is not always directly contingent upon the development of agriculture. It is quite possible that improvement in agricultural production may not lead to the growth of a wide range of non-agricultural activities, especially when non-agricultural incomes are considerably lower in comparison to agricultural incomes. There is either little incentive for the growth of rural non-agricultural activities or those that get established happen to be residual occupations into which people without alternative options are attracted or driven into (Araujo 2003). Commenting on rural enterprises in southern Africa Manona (2001) observed that in most cases non-agricultural activities appear to be a last resort than an attractive alternative. In resource poor agricultural societies of southern Africa the associated negative effects are withdrawal of critical labour inputs from the family farm (de-agrarianisation), while positive effects may include the alleviation of income and credit constraints. It obvious now that de-agrarianisation is subject to reversibility, that is, a reversibility between farm and non-farm livelihood strategies at households level (re-agrarianisation) (Yaro 2006). According to this perspective, livelihood adaptation (implying diversification into new or secondary livelihood activities) involves not just a move from the farm to the non-farm sector, but also sometimes intensification of effort in either the farm or non-farm sector. The actual experiences are subject to variations of economic, social, environmental and political nature. The next chapter delves into variations founded on the social construction of gender relations.

Notes

[1] Much of the use of the livelihood framework has been among development agencies, in particular non-governmental organizations (NGOs)- Department for International Development (DFID) and CARE. The Department for International Development (DFID) livelihoods framework present people as having livelihood assets (financial capital, human capital, social capital, physical capital and natural capital) which they put to use in strategies in order to achieve certain outcomes. The strategies are then associated with various 'livelihoods outcomes': more income, increased wellbeing, reduced vulnerability, improved food security and more sustainable use of natural resource base (Scoones 1998). The use of the sustainable livelihood framework, as a policy tool has recently become problematic, and some scholars have opted to detach their analysis from the prevailing policy discourse, in particular, the tendency in livelihoods research for household assets to be treated as synonymous with various forms of 'capital', and for both assets and capital to be 'torn out of their relational context in the shift to the language of neo-classical economics to explore livelihoods (Francis and Murry 2002). The challenge has been with defining, measuring and delineating various forms of capital assets. Also social capital may mediate access to other assets, in particular access to natural resources and credit where social relationships are pretty important just as social capital in participatory activities could be hijacked by elites.

[2] National Archives of Malawi: NS/3/3/2 Domasi Paper No. 2: An Area Assessment cited in Hirschmann and Vaughan 1984.

[3] See Government Notice No.52 of 20 May 1978) or Hansard Debates of Parliament, 27 March 1978, pp.1000ff). Chirwa, W., Patel, N. and Kanyongolo, E. *Democracy Report for Malawi* http://www.afrimap.org/english/images/documents/file42286243aa6ff.pdf

[4] LADDER Village Report No. 26 Katanda Village, Malawi March 2002 website: http://www.uea.ac.uk/polopoly_fs/1.1007!vr26%20-%20katanda.pdf

[5]Source: LADDER Village Report No. 22 Lumwira Village, Malawi February 2002 website: http://www.uea.ac.uk/polopoly_fs/1.1007!vr22%20-%20lumwira.pdf

[6] FewsNet 'Malawi Food Security Update' October 2007. http://www.fews.net/docs/Publications/Malawi_200710en.pdf

171

[7] Personal experience and also reported in the village I conducted previous studies.

Chapter Eight

Perspectives on gender and development

Gender refers to social categories of being male and female and how they are related one to the other in a variety of ways not just to interactions between individual men and women in the sphere of personal relationships and in terms of biological reproduction. This chapter demonstrates that gender inclusion is a step in the right direction towards correcting various anomalies experienced in agricultural and non-agricultural pursuits and in participatory development. Absence of inclusion compromises effectiveness of development effort and it is one of the underlying causes of uncertainty and various manifestations of poverty, for instance, food insecurity, unemployment and inequality. This is a call for effective empowerment of both women and men in order to accelerate socioeconomic transformation.

Gender and gender relations

Gender is generally understood as a concept of classification and of being male and female (Hendry 2008:30). In this sense gender is socially constructed. Unlike sex which is more of a biological condition, gender encompasses a diversity of social interactions among men and women other than biological characteristics associated with the sex of individuals. It is better appreciated in relation to social relations through which social categories of male and female are related one to the other in a variety of ways not just to interactions between individual men and women, for example, in the sphere of personal relationships or in terms of biological reproduction.

Gender relations are played in all aspects of social life, principally in and through hierarchies that define individual and coordinated access to resources required for production purposes, in the distribution of rewards or remuneration for work, distribution of income and power, and participation in institutions set up for the reproduction and advancement of society; such as education, cultural, political and religious activities and establishments. Considering diverse ways in which gender interests permeate social life gender cannot be ignored in establishing people's behaviour and the outcomes of any social interaction (Pearson (2000). The core concern in this chapter is gender relations as applied to rural development practice; hence the focus on agriculture, non-agricultural activities and participatory development.

A critical trajectory in development theory and practice is female subordination and unequal allocation of resources, opportunities and benefits of work along gender lines. Unequal allocations show that few women are emancipated; many remain chained to custom, practices and work ethics which preserve and anchor their supposedly subordinate status. Women constitute more than one half of the populations of many developing countries but men command disproportionate share of resources (land in particular), employment opportunities, enrolment in education institutions, and then occupy most managerial and decision-making positions both in public and private sectors. Three common themes in the literature on gender and development are presented as discussed in Boserup (1970), Momsen (1991),

174

Braig (2000), Pearson (2000) and Sikod (2007). Firstly, different societies have established division of labour by sex though the categories may not be universal and eventually falling apart. Secondly, women's role in development can be better appreciated by unveiling gender roles in the home and how such roles are also played outside the home. Thirdly, as a result of the first two factors, development has differential impact on women and men and the impact on women has with few exceptions generally been negative. A critique of grand development theories is followed by the discussion on lack of gender inclusion in some development programmes.

Gender in development paradigms

Original conceptualizations of theories of development such as modernization and dependency treated gender as a residual factor (Synder and Tadesse 1995). Modernization emphasizes the contrast between modern and progressive and traditional and backward societies. Modern societies were capitalist, industrialized, advanced economies, synonymous with the West, while traditional societies were peripheral and perhaps non-capitalist, non-industrial, less advanced where traditional values, traditional social structures and institutions including extended family relations, animist religions, pre-capitalist economies and economies of affection, non-western education and non-progressive/ liberal political systems, just to mention the most significant ones, hampered completely progress and development. Development was next to impossible if not based on diffusion and adoption of modern values, capital, technology and political institutions from the

West. In a bid to modernize traditional societies in the developing world, Western education institutions, scientific knowledge and technology, political and religious institutions, capital in the form of aid and direct foreign investment (DFI) were to be transferred to the developing nations. Several critical voices including that of Easter Boserup, Asoka Bandarage and others have showed from the very onset that the benefits of new opportunities introduced in developing countries have more often than not accrued to men. For instance, men have access to more lucrative and prestigious jobs in the formal economy while women have been relegated to least productive and least paid activities for different reasons that include prejudices about gender difference.

The challenge as Momsen (1991) saw it, not in developing countries only, although there have been cases of women power in different ages and societies; there is evidence that no society in the world ever provide women equal status with men. Hence, in the process of modernization development fails to recognize fully and systematically the contribution of women and in turn the effect of the development process on them. Even where this is acknowledged and gender mainstreaming is mentioned as on the top of the development agenda, rhetoric is not always matched with concrete action. With respect to efforts to improve agricultural production, modernization does not simply overlook a good deal that women do, including production within the home, but also does not take full account for the ambiguous impact of development upon women (Foster-Carter 1985 for an earlier critique; Sikod 2007).

In the 1960s modernization theory began to be challenged by the dependency theory whose major premise had been that global capitalism from colonial to neo colonial regimes and of late globalization operate to under develop the developing countries (Frank 1992 for a thorough treatise of dependency theory). The core-periphery paradigm and other similar expressions like metropolis-satellite relations, capture the degree of exploitation endured by poor countries over a long period through uneven economic, political and power relations. For Africa, evidence dates back to the slave trade era through colonialism to the unequal trade regimes and post-independence political interference. In the wake of continued exploitation, developing countries of Africa, Asia and South America have been calling for a new international economic order (NIEO), hoping to placate the tide of dependency. Recent anti-globalization and anti-free trade campaigns (during World Trade Organization (WTO) and United Nations summits) illustrate the dissatisfaction of representatives of civil society groups and the business elites from the developing world over the global economic and political order that entrenches subordination. Could the same be said about the relationship between men and women? Dependency theory fails to relate the external relations of structural dependency to basic dependent relationships within the home and work place affecting women.

In most development endeavours in Africa, males are the authority figures, males make decisions and males get what they want often at the expense of other men and very often at the expense of women. The situation of rural women is complicated by dependent development, for instance, through transfers of capital, technology and values from developed societies and the unequal relations magnified by urban bias. What might be disheartening is that many are too docile and less likely to push for dramatic changes, and where change seems to be happening at a faster pace it is because the former colonial powers or proxy agents have insisted on mainstreaming gender in development often as a precondition for development funding. The following section examines the imbalances in agriculture and non-agricultural activities.

Unequal relations, unequal outcomes

World Bank Sector Paper on Rural Development conceptualized rural development as a strategy designed to improve the economic and social life of a specific group of people- the rural poor. Robert Chambers went further to identify the rural poor as the small-scale producers, tenants, the landless and women (Chambers 1983). The mention of women as a special category of the rural poor reflects the general view that women are a disadvantaged group. This is true for women headed households and equally so for women and girls in male headed households. The mention of rural economies is also pertinent given that rural economic organization provides many opportunities for appreciation of gender relations in situ. Focusing on farming as a major economic activity in many rural areas, for instance, it is adequate to illustrate the unequal relations between men and women. Experiences among farming communities in different countries of the developing world will be cited in order to emphasize that the challenge of mainstreaming gender in development practice is spatially diffused. Few examples from Malawi will be used due to paucity of suitable reference materials.

The lack of information on Malawi is more connected with its political history. For over 30 years following self-rule, the head of state self-styled himself protector and guardian of all women. Then to talk and position women as an oppressed social category could have invited the wrath of the autocratic state and the patriarch. It was enough to acknowledge challenges of poverty generally, but to consider that women's labour and time were exploited could have been tantamount to working against the state. The regime exploited the situation so well such that women and men generally would not acknowledge publicly that women were not getting a fair take in development, not to mention in politics, agricultural projects, education, health and social welfare. The transition to multiparty democracy opened up avenues for self-actualization, at least as manifested by the mushrooming of organizations promoting women's rights, women empowerment, gender equality and rights of the girl child; led mostly by educated urban based women activists. The drive to improve the good of the girl child in education has been one of the areas of interest attracting international donor support. Most political parties that have emerged since the return to multiparty politics have not embraced gender equality wholeheartedly. Gender equality is exploited by individual political actors when canvassing for votes and specifically by female candidates vying for political positions. Often the point of reference has been the SADC agreement setting aside 30% of decision making positions for women, but recently uprated to the 50:50 campaign for all elected positions in local government and parliamentary representation. Why it cannot be 52% or more for Malawi, given the demographic trends, is not reflected upon for political convenience. Otherwise, the need to apply the same to all spheres of life is not advocated for.

Gender equality is but a banner for elite women, those who are by and large already entangled with men and patriarchy over resources at household and national level. At the domestic level, other than the drive against gender based domestic violence, emphasis has tended to narrow down to inheritance laws. The missing ingredient is lack of emphasis on virtues of hard work for boys and girls, men and women and individuals whether they are single or married. The implication for perennial problems of inheritance is obvious. The suggestion by Simone de Beauvoir on the French society of her time is pertinent: 'As long as complete economic equality is not realized in society and as long as the mores authorize woman to profit as wife or mistress from the privileges held by certain men, so long will her dream of unearned success remain and hamper her own accomplishments' (de Beauvoir 1949:388).

With regard to agriculture, it is acknowledged that women are the backbone of the sector. In an earlier study Carr (1991) reported that women in Malawi do approximately 50 – 70 of all farming activities that include planting, weeding, fertilizer application and harvesting. Yet, decision making generally rests with men. Men make decisions on whether to grow cash crops or food crops, type of technologies to be used, size of production, and when and where to buy farm inputs and when and where to sell the farm outputs, especially for cash crops and where lucrative markets are not within the locality. The latitude for women participation is circumscribed to decisions on intercropping, which may not provide financial benefits. With regard to land ownership, notwithstanding differences between matrilineal and patrilineal customary arrangements, data on ownership of rural land/farms obtained from the National Census of Agriculture and Livestock (NACAL) of 2007 showed that there were 6.7 million plots in Malawi, out of which 4.4 million were operated by males and 2.3 million were operated by females (Government of Malawi and National Statistics Office 2012). With respect to urban plots and houses as well as livestock ownership IHS 2 (2005) depicts disparities between women and men. A conventional reason for the difference is that men have more financial capacity than women to procure, own and operate on farms/plots, urban land and houses. Only those women (about 20% of the total) are able to buy urban land and houses and these are in the working class or successful business women (Government of Malawi and National Statistics Office 2012).

For various countries it has been shown that statistical evidence on gender roles are often very unreliable since it is sometimes culturally problematic and sometimes unacceptable for women to claim that they work in agriculture and for census takers to record women as having an economic role (Momsen 1991). Women are in such rural areas regarded as housewives and domestic workers regardless of their active participation in crop and animal husbandry. Yet, it is the same women who have been known generally for producing an average of 60% of food consumed in developing countries. Although estimates vary across countries women grow some 80% of food in Africa, do 50% of animal husbandry and close to 100% of food processing, preservation and preparation. A relatively recent study confirms this status quo. Women perform about 90% of the work of processing food crops and providing household water and fuel wood, 80% of the work related to food storage, 90% of the work of hoeing and weeding, and 60% of the work of harvesting and marketing (Sikod 2007). No studies have to date contradicted these estimates. The paradox is, given that food is one of the most important commodities in world trade and with women producing over half of world food, is it justifiable to say that women generally are marginalized? One would have to look into the gender division of labour and the allocation of land and supporting services to farming such as new agricultural technology, agricultural credit and extension services.

On labour allocation, agricultural tasks continue to be defined and allocated in terms of socially determined sex roles. The gender division of agricultural tasks, for instance, men would undertake 'heavy' physical labour of land preparation and activities involving movements to distant locations such as livestock herding or trading of farm output while women would carry out repetitive and time consuming tasks including weeding or tasks which are located close to the home. The division of labour sometimes extends to the type of crops produced. Whenever there is a gendered crop production, crops regarded as ideal for men tend to be cash crops like tobacco, cocoa, sisal, just to name some; while crops like millet, cassava, sorghum, potatoes are regarded as ideal crops for women (Chambers 1983; Momsen 1991) and often produced to satisfy subsistence requirements. These aspects mean that women are in principle marginalized from the cash economy, although it has been observed that women dominate in trading of food in rural markets. However, where a married woman collaborates with her husband in producing cash crops like tobacco, cotton, sugarcane, tea and coffee; the income from such crops is often controlled and spend by the husband. Evidence from Africa indicates that in many cases many men do not spend earnings on improving health and nutrition of their families, rather on luxury consumer goods, alcohol and on other women (Momsen 1991). In India, 80 to 100% of women's wage income is devoted to family maintenance, whereas men commit only between 40 and 90% of their earnings (World Bank 1990). In short, the benefits of rising from cash crop production may accrue entirely to men.

The bias is reinforced by programs to modernize agriculture, for example, agricultural research and extension, new technology and credit. In agricultural research bias is amply magnified as crop research, priority, prestige and promotion have often been on export crops, grown usually on plantations by large farmers, the better off small-scale farmers and men rather than women. As Robert Chambers observed, it is only in the last three decades that international agricultural centres have started recognizing and directing attention to crops such as millet, sorghum etc., that are generally associated with women and produced for subsistence (Chambers 1983). On the other hand, dissemination of supporting agricultural extension messages has been biased the other way. Often agricultural development officials are mostly men even in the societies where farming is carried out mostly by women (Mathur 1986 for an earlier account).

The marginalization of women in agriculture is heightened by the introduction of agricultural credit. For example, women had no access to credit under the Sierra Leone integrated agricultural development project because it was felt that their fields were too small to make good use of credit. In Senegal's and Gambia's rural development projects of the 1980s, credit was channelled through cooperatives in which women could not become members (World Bank 1988). In situations characterized by high levels of male labour migration, women farmers have generally been left out of extension services where extension workers focus on the head of the household (African Development Bank 1995). Furthermore, female farmers have been neglected by male agricultural extension workers as agricultural extension programmes are sometimes geared towards men even where many if not most cultivators are women (Chambers 1983; World Bank 1990). In Malawi participation of women in agricultural extension has been low because traditionally women would not mix freely with males. As a result, the persistent challenges of low food production and soaring food insecurity are closely linked to limited access to extension services and modern agricultural technologies largely associated with social exclusion of women.

On the same account, male extension workers who are in the majority of this cadre of agricultural professionals concentrate on male farmers because of the socio-cultural coding. It is imperative that extension work should be oriented towards farmers of all categories without discrimination on the basis of gender. The result of such a change would still be dismal if women do not enjoy equal access to land and credit without the usual requirement of collateral.

Access to productive resources and marketing opportunities is particularly skewed against female-headed households. The World Bank's *World Development Report* (1990) cites a village study in India's Uttar Pradesh state where the most disadvantaged groups happened to be landless casual labourers for whom work is not always available on a regular basis and households without an able-bodied male. Often households with both these characteristics tend to be extremely poor as they have very few opportunities for raising income. In Southern Africa, female-headed households constitute a considerable proportion of farm households. Here, it implies that many households would therefore operate outside the market. These are the majority of women headed households who produce non-tradable food staples for household consumption, with a significantly small if not negligible 'marketable surplus'. Being in this state is thus to be considered a double tragedy. Difficulties in gaining access to productive resources compound the problem as the majority of those not directly owning land cannot respond to price incentive by allocating land to lucrative crops or expanding acreage. Even where women's access to land is guaranteed, gross output of women farmers is in many cases rather low. This has been demonstrated by one of the studies in Kenya, for instance. Here the gross value of output per hectare for men was at one time 18% higher than for women. However, it was then noted that if women could be given the same capital endowments and use the same amount of factors and inputs as men, the value of their output could increase by at least 22% (Pellekaan and Hartnett 2000). For this very reason poverty is more pronounced in female-headed households and it can thus

185

be attributed to cultural practices which hand over wealth and property to men. As one woman in Kagera district, Tanzania, once put it: 'men own everything because when they were born they just found it like that'. In this part of Tanzania it was then noted that male-headed households owned an average of 6.08 acres of land while female-headed households possessed 3.74 acres of land only (Nayaran 1997).[1]

Impacts are more pronounced where agriculture development plans and programmes ignore or disregard the needs of women completely, common in situations where development plans and programmes are formulated by men for men. Programmes like changes in land-use rights, introduction of cash crops, as explained above, and subsidies and extension advice would thus favour men. Women in such instances might not be entitled to credit and might be systematically excluded from projects involving mechanization. It is on record that mechanization of agriculture provides jobs for men but often at the expense of a large number of female agricultural labourers. This happens without providing women with alternative avenues for earning income (Burkey 1993). The introduction of mechanical rice hullers in rice production in Java displaced women labour since men were employed to run the machines. The general rule has been that when time saving devices are introduced, tasks they are designed for tend to be taken over by men. Women lose access to traditional sources of income. Such a development enhances male prestige on one hand and reduce the status of women on the other hand within the household and in society. Likewise, the restructuring of development activities leads to increasing prestige of men who are associated with capital intensive and 'modern' technology while women's status is lowered by structural exclusion. Economic and cultural powerlessness of women, 'invisibility' of rural women's productive activities, and male dominance in planning agencies have been major underlying challenges. Targeting women for special action has been problematic also. 'Women projects' isolated from the rest of development planning may suffer the debilitating challenges of poor funding and of not being taken seriously.[2]

The Southern Africa region has a long history of female headed households due to male labour migration to the mines in South Africa and to urban areas, which means that farming has been predominantly done by women and children (Low 1986; Selolwane 1992). As the main product of agriculture is food, in societies where small-scale producers have adopted cash cropping, the gender division of labour takes the form of a gendered crop production. As women grow food crops while men grow the cash crops, although the pattern is not always universal, a pro-food strategy that ignores the contribution of women may not effectively address the challenge of food security (Burkey 1993).

It is beyond dispute that gender balance is a critical missing ingredient. Promoting women's productivity would directly contribute to household's welfare much more than the current pro-male and anti-female bias. The unfortunate long-term effect of pro-male bias is the 'feminization of poverty' (Bandarage 1984:499), a scenario in which women and daughters are worse off than men, spouses and sons. The dilemma of women coffee farmers in Tanzania provide vivid illustration of subordination, marginalization and feminization of poverty:

> 'Women work on the village farm but very few men do. Women weed the coffee; they pick coffee, pound it and spread it to dry. They pack and weigh it. But when the crop gets a good price, the husband takes all the money. He gives each of his wives 200 Shillings and climbs on a bus the next morning, ... most go to town and stay in a boarding house until they are broke. Then they return and attack their wives saying 'why haven't you weeded the coffee'. This is the big slavery' (statement by a woman activist, in Bernstein 1992d:79).

Bases of gender inequality

In many societies kinship ties play a major influence in the mobilization of labour as shown by Terry's (1972) 'lineage mode of production' and Malinowski (1921) 'Tribal economy', in contrast to Bücher (1911) 'Independent Domestic Economy' (Wilk 1996; Narotzky 1997). The household is an important unit of analysis in production systems characterised by domestic mode of production or householding. A household regulates access to land and labour. The definition of the household is subject to cross-cultural variations. The western concept of a household and of gender roles do not correspond to those in sub-Saharan Africa.[3]

Claude Meillassoux argued that kinship is one of the ways by which elders in 'traditional' egalitarian communities and households exploit other members. His study in West African examined how in the 'domestic mode of production' elderly men exploit younger men and women by controlling labour, bride wealth, lineage membership and the marriage of daughters. According to Wilk, 'whereas in the capitalist mode of production, wealth is based in the control of property, in the domestic mode, wealth is based on the control of people. The elders decide who gets married to whom, what lineage children belong to, and who gets to farm which piece of land. In the lineage mode of production the control of economic surplus is achieved through control of custom and family connections, rather than through wages or tribute' (Wilk 1996:93).

Studies carried out before and after the 1990s in the Andean region have demonstrated how household members and households units rarely function as paragons of harmony or as units of convergent interests, but often as units with divergent interests (Zoomers 1999). Interest in different activities also appear in Andean studies which have shown that often relations shift between cooperation, conflict and bargaining. Bargaining and conflict become urgent when households are adjusting to extreme conditions of resource insufficiency, unfavourable markets and the insensitive state (Mayer 2002). Furthermore, although transformation in the mode of production has direct effect on adults, its impact needs to be examined from a cross generation perspective. In a world replete with cross cultural interactions children may grow up with different sets of values and beliefs, a phenomenon that is associated with exposure to new ideas through schooling, the media, and work or social experiences outside one's own community.

Severity of impact may vary from place to place. However, women as the subject in gender discourse in developing countries head smaller households than those headed by men, have higher dependency ratios, own less land or fewer livestock (Woodson 2007) which imply a weaker position to farm than are male-headed households. There is need for caution as this position could be over simplifications of diverse and complex situations. As Polly Hill once remarked for Africa:

> In Africa there is not only a division of labour by sex and age but also a broader division of economic spheres. Men and women- and often children- separately control productive resources, take partly independent decisions, manage personal incomes, assume different responsibilities and favour different investments. Their liens on each other's resources, labour and income are so complex that the outcome of 'household' decisions is difficult to predict and even to describe systematically' (Hill (1975) cited in Guyer 1986:93).

Although gender division of labour is a universal phenomenon, the actual divisions are actually not universal. Haddad and Hoddinott (1994) observed in Cote d'Ivoire gendered crop allocation. Income from 'male crops' such as coffee, cocoa, tends to be put to different uses than income from 'female crops' such as maize, bananas, sugarcane, coconut etc. Although this is not consistent with a unitary model of the household, where all household members have the same purse or utility function or where a 'dictator' makes decisions for everyone, it is however consistent with the more general collective model where individuals may bargain over the household allocation (Duflo and Udry 2003). Apparently, in many cases in West Africa men and women control separate incomes as Duflo and Udry (2003) show on account of the earlier work of Guyer (1980: 369 -70):

'Men control their own cash income, and the kinds of legitimate demands a wife can make can be quite limited. A Yoruba wife can expect her husband to provide the basic staples of the diet, housing, and other more irregular support depending on how much domestic work she devotes to him (......) Beti wives remain farmers throughout their lives. Before the recent expansion of food sales they used to depend on their husbands for all major cash expenses, but neither in theory nor in day-to day life is a wife's right to her own share of her husband's cash income guaranteed (......) Family welfare and risk avoidance are probably improved by the family labour force having a variety of occupations which cater to different markets, but the need in bad times and the opportunity in good times for a woman to earn an independent income originate in a domestic organization with limited income sharing'

In Ghana (the former Gold Coast) the introduction of cocoa as a cash crop led many women to establish their own farms, rather than labour on the farm of a husband (Allman 1996).[4]

Gender and rural non-agricultural activities

Statistics on different levels of involvement of women and men in rural non-farm employment suggest that women do not participate on equal terms. In rural areas of Mali the participation rate of women was in the 1990s at 16% only to 84% for men (Hussein and Nelson 1998).

Rural African women's lack of involvement in cash-earning activities was generally assumed by donor agencies throughout the 1970s and 1980s. The prominence of income diversification studies over the last two decades overturned this assumption. Rural women are earning cash income, although it is from generally less remunerative work compared to that of men. Women remain largely restricted to income-earning activities based on home-making skills. A number of studies have shown that women gravitate towards homestead based occupations such as handicrafts, textile making, gathering and selling firewood and stones, manual work in brick fields and earthwork on roads and forms of construction, in rice mills, as well as domestic helpers (Mallorie 2003). In non-Muslim study sites for the DARE survey, beer brewing and sales of prepared food were usually major income earners among women (Bryceson, 1999).

In female-headed households women have a larger role. Generally, the quest to meet survival requirements for the poor households often demands that women take a greater role in income generation. In rural Uganda, for example, women participate more actively in crop farming than men, whilst the latter are more involved in non-farm activities (Wandschneider 2003). Men show greater propensity to diversify into non-traditional occupations such as carpentry and construction, whereas women in traditional activities such as handicrafts and alcohol brewing. However, female-heads face an advantageous position vis-à-vis married woman in terms of decision-making power and control over assets required for income-generating activities in the non- farm sector (Smith 2001). In the case of Zimbabwe, men are able to avail themselves of diversification opportunities that are not open to women due to constraints associated with accessing credit. Women are reputed as efficient in paying loans; ironically they have the hardest time in securing loans without collateral, male consent, and security against the loan (Mutangadura 2005).

Gender and the participatory development paradigm

Development thinking has been influenced by the participatory paradigm founded on devolution of decision making power. Failure of externally driven projects or lack of project sustainability, and resource constraints have contributed to popularization of the shift in development thinking and practice (Streeten 1995; Jimu 2008b). Development is considered devoid of meaning if the ultimate stakeholders are passive or on the receiving end. The maxim is that rural communities should be active agents in meeting development needs rather than passive beneficiaries waiting for the largess of the central government or outside agents. In many instances non-governmental organisations (NGOs) are deemed as better placed to facilitate the mobilization of communities than the government (Singh 1999). However, the broader political and economic processes that have made 'participation' such a fashionable issue of late – and not only in Africa; show that, participation is bluntly a result of world-wide spread of neoliberal policies that claim to 'empower' people by withdrawing the state from their lives while imposing on communities an undemocratic non-governmental sector, often bankrolled by opaque transnational agencies (Jimu 2008b). The basic challenge is how 'community development' could possibly be a panacea for socioeconomic progress and empowerment of women when neoliberalism is conspicuously quiet on the socio-cultural and power relations that keep rural communities poor and especially worse for women and children.

Participation requires delimiting the participatory group. In this respect three questions are critical: how should people participate? In what should people participate? Where should people participate (Vyasulu 2002)? To answer these questions, participation requires existences of a participatory group or community. Warburton (1998) suggested that a 'community' relates to two dimensions of 'people' and 'place' given that it emphasizes the relationships among people and between people and the place in which they are located (Worpole and Greenhalgh 1996). A community upon which this contemporary development philosophy is founded could be construed as comprising the web of personal relationships, group networks, as well as traditions and patterns of behaviour most of which develop against the backdrop of that physical locality and its social, economic and political configurations. Emphasizing on the positive side, in this context participation is good for the residents of an area, allowing them as principal stakeholders to influence the future development of their locality. It is to be assumed that the 'good' of the community is intrinsically linked with the social, economic, political and environmental forces through interconnectedness of individuals and the societies or communities to which they belong. Commitment to participation reflects peoples' self-consciousness drawing on that interconnectedness. It needs mentioning, therefore, that the principle of community development has its logical and epistemological basis in social obligations. Participation or self-help spirit is to be inspired by awareness among individuals and the communities they belong to and the recognition that individuals become who they are- agents- through relationship with others (Nyamnjoh 2002:111).

The challenge is: why is participation rarely voluntary and intrinsically derived? Page (2002) notes that in Anglophone Africa, 'community development' is partly based on colonial tradition of 'self-help' which became the main British strategy for implementation of welfare oriented colonial development policy in the 1950s. Malawi shares in this Anglophone colonial tradition. Community development during colonial and post-colonial times has been based on coercion and control (Jimu 2008b).

From the foregoing community participation in rural development does not exist in the abstract. It is defined through specific existing situations, institutions, processes and ideological and cultural factors. It relies on the imposition of traditional social order. Campbell (1995) contends that the ideology of community rests on a triune of the community, the family and the individual, which support traditional hierarchical structures For this reason, the low status of women in most rural societies, role stereotypes and belief that awareness of the needs of the community is greater among women tend to put the burden on women as individuals and groups of individuals involved in participatory development processes (Kaufman 1997b). Within a participatory structure various forms of social inequality and gender oppression are reflected and maintained (Pahl 1995). The inequality and subordination of women in community development manifest itself at decision-making. Men dominate decision-making but contribute little in the implementation process. In most cases, rural development projects reflect the perceptions of men and therefore serve men's interests better than those of women since the way decisions are reached ensures male bias in the design of projects, presumably because of the belief that women's interests, as parts of the male dominated households, are reflected in the interests of husbands and fathers (Oakley and Marsden 1984).

Male bias in community development, as in agricultural development, has been used as an argument to encourage 'targeting' of women, and creation of groups for women only. However, some development projects that target women make the error of assuming that women's labour time is infinitely elastic. Such endeavours tend to put further strains on women's participation (Bernstein 1992). Others, however, have argued that the challenge community work confounds upon women creates opportunities for women's voice and concerns to be heard. Given that rural women are victims of traditions which hinder effective participation in development activities, women's only organizations accord women opportunity and ability to speak out (Rahman 1993). The issue of participation in decision-making is contentious. Does silence of women in mixed meetings always reflect the oppression by men? It has been demonstrated in some cases that women might be silent decision makers.[5] Thus it needs ascertaining whether silence is not due to indoctrination or distortion of perception of social oppression.

Yet, rather than propagating blindly the equalization of treatment, it is also pertinent to acknowledge gender-based differences in interests and priorities. Francis et al. (1996) for instance argue that rural men and women are not homogenous in all aspects. They emphasized the need to consider peculiar needs of women, men and children separately to attain effective participation. In a study on the state, community and local development in Nigeria, Francis et al. observed that sometimes men, women, and young people have different development priorities. Men's priority has always been on access to information about more profitable crops, agricultural credit and extension advice, while women tend to be keen on access to small loans towards food production, which could be repaid in regular instalments, and on domestic water supply. Young people on the other hand are inclined to have credit to enable them start small-scale income generating activities in new non-agricultural occupations. Such variations in expressed needs reflect the different responsibilities and aspirations. Take the example of the shared need for credit. While men, women and young people all yearn for access to credit, it is often for different purposes: commercial agriculture, subsistence agriculture and non-farm investments, respectively. They also note that while all the three groups need water, an improved domestic water supply is a priority for women specifically because in rural areas women are responsible for fetching household water (Francis et al. 1996). The underlying factor is however the gender division of labour or the traditional allocation of tasks, which generally confines women to the production for the homestead (Pellekaan and Hartnett 2000). The gender division of labour extends into the choices that men and women make in public works. The biases and inconsistences are evident in community rural water projects (Cleaver 1994).

Cleaver observed that women dominated community participation in rural water projects in Zimbabwe. For instance, village water point committees are largely composed of women. Emphasis has often been on selecting and training women as committee members and as the main collectors and drawers of water for domestic use. Focusing on women however, ignores the fact that water has multiple uses, just as there are multiple sources, and that the major consumers of water are men. Tasks performed by men like moulding bricks, building houses and herding cattle involve considerable utilization of water. Different water uses have different sources. For some of the uses, rivers or wells are deemed appropriate whereas boreholes are appropriate for domestic uses. Women, children especially daughters, and small animals (goats and donkeys) tend to be the main users of wells whereas boreholes have a greater proportion of male users and cattle, yet management committees for both water sources are composed of women. Water is a complex resource and a focus on one gender category misses the point by overlooking the social dynamics of water usage.

Closing reflections

Given the foregoing discussion, women experience marginalization and near exclusion in many development and economic activities and it is absolute indifference to argue that men and women participate and benefit from development on equal terms. The important points of reference are demarcations between domestic and public spheres or reproductive and productive sectors that are socially and culturally constructed to promote but also justify subordination of women to men. The allocation of housework and childcare to women, for instance, affects women's participation in agriculture, non-agricultural activities, as well as in the formal labour market. Reproductive work is not regarded as work in the sense of not paid for well and quite often where it is paid for wage rates tend to be extremely low.

Braig (2000), however, observes that measures aimed at promoting women's participation sometimes operate to disadvantage women even more. In making women's productive role visible, reproductive and community roles fall by the wayside. Frequently, promotional measures mean a greater workload for workingwomen particularly if the decisive problem of redistribution of reproductive work is not addressed. In addition, women experience dehumanizing treatment in the form of sexual harassment both in the home and at work places. Some male supervisors demand sex in return for job security, promotion, salary increment, training opportunities, just to mention some.

Case studies of community development cited above indicate that women are active agents in rural development. Although their latitude is confined mostly to traditional tasks, it illustrates that there are few areas of rural life in which women are not involved. Yet, a focus on the role of women in community development that confines the status of women to providers of labour lead to situations where women end up doing tasks for rather than with men. Men become a burden on women as Mao, China's Communist leader in the 1950s and

1960s, once put it: 'Chinese men carry the burden of three mountains: oppression from outside, feudal oppression and the burden of their own backwardness. But Chinese women are burdened by four mountains, the fourth being Chinese men' (Burkey 1993:64).

A gender and development approach calls for the extension of participation to involve not just labour input but also ownership of the means of participation, particularly through greater participation in decision-making. Consolidation of democratic ideals may likely turn community development into an instrument through which women and men together create the means to invigorate transformation of rural society, dissolve gender barriers, prejudices and inequalities and the notion of men as the wielders of power (Kaufman 1997a).

There is need for approaches to development that on one hand address practical everyday needs and on the other hand work strategically towards eliminating the hierarchy of genders. Focusing on women should, however, guard against misrepresentation of dependency and exploitation of women. Advocating for the inclusion of women in development without a transformation of the socio-cultural system would overburden women with new tasks.

There are already serious strides in this direction. Among them is the intervention of many multilateral donor organizations, including various agencies of the UN and the European Union (EU), the Department for International Development (DFID), the Canadian International Development agency (CIDA) and Danish Development Agency (DANIDA) and USAID that have mandatory frameworks that include gender inclusiveness.[6] Perhaps, what needs guarding against is turning gender talk and drive into 'a kind of neo-colonial imposition on communities and countries where there are other priorities and other understandings of gender differences and gender roles' (Pearson 2000:285). Transformation of gender relations is essential for the realisation of development goals, one of which is gender equality through empowerment of all women and girls by 2030. This is a call for effective empowerment of both women and men in order to accelerate socioeconomic transformation. It is also a requirement if poverty and inequalities were to be overcome.

Notes

[1] Similar patterns are to be observed in many places with similar customs. However, where customs differ, for instance among matriarchal ethnic groups in Ghana and Central Africa, there are some exceptions to the general rule.

[2] Sometimes the critical challenge has been securing solutions appropriate to a problem. As Momsen (1991) wrote, in many rural areas of the developing world, women's problems require small-scale solutions rather than large scale, high technology or high prestige programmes which do not fit well with government priorities.

[3] Gregory and Altman (1989) suggest that while it is important to define the household, definitions have to be multidimensional with respect to residential, commensal, genealogical, and occupational criteria. As they write there is a need to ascertain by empirical investigation and observation what physical structure constitutes the house and the relations between the people who occupy it. Definitions must further take cognizance of the

change in household composition over time and also cross variations between. The alternative view though not unnecessarily contradictory is provided in Wilk and Netting (1984) cited in Narotzky (1997:115) who suggested that when speaking of a household, it is always important to distinguish between morphology and function. In other words, between what a domestic group is and what it does. Morphology is a material and cultural concept defining the spatial boundaries and binding links between people forming a household, while function relates to the recurring agency among morphologically defined household members. Turning to the notion of function, there is debate on the pattern of change and of the composition of the household through time, what is called the domestic cycle. The notion of domestic cycle suggests that relationships between members of the household are continually being re-negotiated along basic categories of gender and age, which are also cultural and social products (Narotzky 1997:115). Sahlins suggested that in the domestic mode of production decisions are taken primarily with a view toward domestic contentment and for that reason for the benefit of the producers (Sahlins1974). He loosely equates the domestic group of the household to the family, though he acknowledged that production units are not always family like in nature. Where the household is a family system, the forms vary from nuclear to extended, and within the extended category from polygynous through matrilocal, patrilocal, and other arrangements. Each one of these aspects implies differentiated production and consumptions arrangements. Although household members, as would be expected, are mainly kin, other non-kin people may share the same space and linked by other than kinship relationships. Non-kin members may be related to members of a household by wage relations (Narotzky 1997).

[4] A situation in Cote d'Ivoire among the Gouro studied by Meillassoux (1965) provides a sharp contrast between 'appreciated products' (for example yams), ordinary food products, products cultivated by women, and cash crops (Duflo and Udry 2003). 'Appreciated products' are always under the control of the household head for redistribution to the entire household in the form of food. In contrast, the control of cash crops belongs to its producer. Apparently, cash crops and food crops, even when they are cultivated by the same individual, and even when food crops are sold on the market, are not put to the same use: 'In the traditional community, as we have seen, most of the production comes back to producers in the form of food. The rest is incorporated into particular goods, which have a specific role at the time of marriage (...). Everything changes when the products of agriculture are cash crops which can be put to other uses (...).

A greater part of this income disappears into prestige expenditures, especially into investment into houses which are monuments to the glory of their owners.' (Meillassoux (1965:335) cited in Duflo and Udry 2003).

[5] This view was advanced by a study of bee keeping in Gambia by Mohammed (1989). Field staff felt that women were not participating in decision-making because of fear of men. Often women would state that 'when the men speak, they speak on our behalf'. Such an answer did not only seem unconvincing but was seen by the development agents as a cultural barrier hampering democratic and effective decision-making. Mohammed observed that sometimes development staff fails to realize that in rural areas the social relationship between men and women is characterized by mutual respect. He further argued that women have a great deal of authority, which is usually exercised behind closed doors. While men make their voices heard during meetings, the women are the ones behind the decisions made at night time or just behind the scenes and behind closed doors.

[6] There have been United Nations (UN) conferences of women in Mexico (1975), Copenhagen (1980), Nairobi (1985) and Beijing (1995). These conferences have produced blueprints for eliminating discrimination against women and for ensuring that women's interests and needs are well reflected in the global agenda for development. International development conferences, including the UN Conference on Environment and Development (UNCED) in Rio (1992), the International Human Rights Conference in Vienna (1993), the Population and Development Conference in Cairo (1994), the Social Summit in Copenhagen (1995), and the Habitat Summit in Ankara (1996), all advocated the inclusion of gender in the development process.

204

Chapter Nine

Moving in Circles

Moving in circles is not a natural condition. Indicators include pervasive poverty, food insecurity, liquidation of productive assets like land, and low livelihood diversification. In the midst of these challenges uncertainty stands out as a cost as it is also the catalyst. There is need to reflect on the ways uncertainty and under development are magnified through the lenses of liberalization of economies, currencies and opportunistic privatization of state institutions. Unfortunately, these have become covert ways of plundering the state through corrupt acquisition of assets. The long-term impacts are quite obvious; poverty, inequality, low levels of employment and low investment in long term development.

Two steps forward and three steps backward

Previous chapters have demonstrated the impacts of lack of development and progress as pervasive poverty, low income levels, food insecurity, liquidation of productive assets like land and low livelihood diversification. These conditions anchor uncertainty as they are critical indicators of development or its lack thereof in developing countries.

Plans, policies, programmes and projects formulated to deal with these undesirable conditions but which encourage tried and failed courses of action and those that constrain economic growth and defy sound social and economic rationality are counter-productive, retrogressive and barrier to achieving aspirations of meaningful economic take off, growth and development. This is true for policies formulated ostensibly to promote economic progress and to benefit the rural or urban poor or women and the youth, but which ultimately benefit the urban elite, men and the older generations, high ranking politicians and business associates. Such policies cannot be said to be good even if there is significant growth in gross domestic income.

Malawi clocked 50 years of independence in July 2014. Malawi had committed to achieving Millennium Development Goals (MDGs), that is, to reduce by half extreme poverty and hunger by 2015. Since the late 1980s Malawi government has been pursuing structural adjustment programmes (SAPs). Malawi's poverty reduction strategy adopted in early 2000s, between 2002 – 2005 to be precise, included measures prioritizing economic growth, infrastructural development, and the provision of basic social services in health and education(Government of Malawi 2002b). Other notable measures in the 1990s included the Poverty Alleviation Program (PAP) (1994) and more recently the Malawi Growth and Development Strategy (MGDS I & II) (hyped as Malawi's homegrown version of MGDs) extending for two five years periods from 2006 through 2011 and from 2011 through 2016. Malawi remains one of the poorest countries in the world.This chapter interrogates the status quo especially as it relates to challenges with transforming development rhetoric into concrete action. Subsequent reflections will revolve around the following questions: What has been happening? Why? Who has gained; who has lost? Does it matter? If so, what can be done about it, and by whom? (Stilwell 2002:4). As Stilwell aptly put it, to answer 'what is happening' requires a careful definition of the process and appreciation of the interaction between local and global dimensions.

Recollecting half-century of development rhetoric

It is confounding that half a century after independence low development and high poverty levels could be attributed to geographical and historical accidents; including unpredictable and harsh climatic regimes, low endowment of mineral resources, harsh realities instigated by seven and a half decades of colonial rule, half a century of neo-colonial domination, land alienations and the land locked situation. Writing about the transition from colonial to postcolonial period, Pryor (1990) argued that for 75 years British colonialists had neglected Malawi referring to it as an 'imperial slum', 'the Ireland of Central Africa-poor, scenic, and with a ready supply of exportable labour'. It was felt, in other words, that Malawi had literary little potential for economic growth and development. Also, at the time of independence many people familiar with the economic situation also spoke of the lack of economic viability of an 'empty government' in a nation with an 'empty economy' (Pryor 1990:39).

Given that in the mid-1960s Malawi had, not in the metaphorical sense, an empty economy, is it not over pessimistic to argue that Malawi has not made some headway in development? Under Dr Banda's autocratic regime Malawi managed to put up a road network, a network of district hospitals and health centres countrywide, encouraged a estate farming, funded several small and medium scale irrigation and settlement schemes and of course a new capital city with credit lines from diverse sources. The last two decades of multiparty democracy have been challenging, and for critics a period of gross maladministration. Has Malawi failed dismally?

It appears that central to the problem is that while government development strategy in the first three decades of independence was articulated as agricultural oriented, the first ten years of the new democratic dispensation were a period of experimentation. Under accelerated liberalization of the 1990s, everything passed for good as 'poverty alleviation'. Policy makers failed to identify the sectors that could play a leading role in the poverty amelioration strategy. Instead, corruption was nurtured at all levels for some out of sheer greed yet for others as a way of making ends meet. Various programmes initiated ostensibly to alleviate poverty turned into avenues for corruption. It is now possible to appreciate demerits of peripheral position in the global political economy and of irresponsible leadership. Yet, indebtedness and corruption cannot be blamed on bad soil or unpredictable weather conditions. These are facets of poor governance, inappropriate policies and deficient leadership.

While acknowledging the global tyranny, group self-interests of selfish leaders, representing narrow interests continue to make the poor vulnerable to global imperatives. In other words drawing on Kings Phiri, emeritus professor of African and Black History at the University of Malawi, how much nourishment and health can a toddler be expected to get from sharing a plate with a gluttonous and overbearing adult (Phiri 2001)? Three major themes are crucial to unravelling the persistence of moving in circles: economic and market liberalization and the liberalization of the exchange rate, and the 'liberalization' of corruption.

Politics of economic liberalizations

Economic liberalization entails deregulation, rolling back state control of the economy and elimination of various restrictions on commerce along the model propagated by the IMF and World Bank since the 1980s and known as structural adjustment programmes (SAPs). Since the 1980s Malawi has been on and off the adjustment path (Harrigan 2001; Stambuli 2002). The process accelerated in the mid-1990s with the privatization of state controlled corporations and the restructuring of the agricultural sector. To date, conspicuous result felt by poor people at the grassroots include effects of the withdrawal of subsidies on essential commodities like farm inputs and accelerated in flows of goods and services and more recently of people largely of west and east African and Asian origin. One of the vibrant markets in Mzuzu is named Taifa market after the Tanzanian traders who were at one point in the majority and for the dominance of merchandise imported from and through Tanzania. In all the major cities and towns, and some rural trading centres, Chinese traders are eventually displacing local traders. Most of the items of trade are imported from China. The effect is that the importance of South Africa and India as sources of most of hardware and manufactured imports has actually collapsed. The quality of imported items has in turn actually plummeted. The merits of the liberalization of the economy are yet to be fully realized.

Every year producers of cotton, tobacco and maize complain about unfair prices. Imported inputs are sold at prices that are exorbitant by far. As early as 2001 The United Nations Conference on Trade and Development (UNCTAD)

(2001) in its report titled *Economic Development in Africa: performance, prospects and policy issues* concluded that:

> 'However, while structural adjustment programmes have been applied more intensely and frequently in Africa than in any other developing region, barely any African country has exited from such programmes with success, establishing conditions for rapid, sustained economic growth. This is true not only for countries which are said to have slipped in the implementation of stabilization and adjustment programmes (the so-called non-adjusters or bad-adjusters), but also most of the core-and good-adjusters.' (UNCTAD 2001:5)

Malawi is an example of bad-adjusters not because the poor have been resisting adjustments, but because of the leadership within and the logic of the international political economy. Sometimes the leaders have perceived IMF or World Bank intervention as unnecessary and unacceptable challenge to realization of domestic economic and their own political goals. Malawi has been on and off the structural adjustment path and for different reasons could not be expected to come out successful in a programme that has failed good and core adjusters. Contrary to expectations, it is spurious to argue that all Malawians have effectively lost. Liberalization has expanded opportunities for some categories of people, especially the educated and politically connected. In some cases the advantages have made liberalization appear state sponsored corruption, hence necessitating the need to interrogate the integrity and calibre of leaders entrusted to steer social and economic transformation.

In the 1990s privatization of state companies resulted in job redundancies that worsened the economic prospects of employees in an economy already burdened with high unemployment and underemployment. The pre-liberalization businesses were exposed to increasing competition from imported, often cheap and inferior goods. While manufacturing grew by 3.3% per annum between 1987 and 1995, between 1996 and 1999 it stagnated and several industries either stopped domestic production or closed completely. Statistics show that in 1999 the main player in the textile industry shrank to 44% of its 1996 level, shedding over 70% of its workforce and in September 2003 it was sold out to an Indian owned company at a price well below the market value of its assets. Is it not paradoxical that privatization could mean selling state enterprises at giveaway prices to foreign business persons?

There were and there are still some politicians for whom privatization and currently private-public partnerships (PPPs) are opportunity for personal accumulation of wealth so much so that the processes involved are actually less about liberalization and more about looting. To such individuals, liberalization in whatever guise is an avenue not only for personal enrichment but also a way by which big men employ traditional forms of patronage and clientelism (Morris 2000) to access state resources to reward old or win new supporters. In general, liberalization is accepted because it facilitates a deliberate policy of spoils and plunder of public coffers by the ruling elite. Malawi is home to entrepreneurs thriving due to politics of greed coated in the language of rolling back state involvement in the economy.

While the protagonists of economic liberalization abroad and optimists at home have blamed inefficient production systems for the decline or death of local entrepreneurship, they have also let unscathed global forces preying on and marginalizing the economic prospects of low income citizens. Effectively these are the effects of the tendency of economic liberalization in developing countries to expose domestic firms to competition from imports before they are able to increase efficiency and competitiveness (Morrissey and Filatotchev 2000). Free flows of foreign capital, goods and competitive entrepreneurial spirit have been let loose to pillage local entrepreneurial spirit aptly in a manner described by Taylor (2001) as the subordination of domestic economies to the perceived exigencies of the global economy. The prevailing political economy reflects inter-country and regional differentials and unequal capacities to tap the advantages offered by globalization or meet the challenges it engenders (Akokpari 2000). It is for these reasons that measures to liberalize the agricultural sector have not in any significant way benefited the poor, in particular the rural poor. Instead liberalization continues to have damaging impacts on input supply, marketing, and provision of credit services. Removal of subsidies and reducing the role of the state exercised through Agricultural Development and Marketing Corporation (ADMARC) in the 1990sled to a boom in private firms, local and foreign, involved in the supply of farm inputs and the purchase of farm outputs. While the number of players has increased, accessibility measured by affordability has not improved. Most private traders are interested in buying farm output and not supplying farm inputs. Most private traders and firms are driven by short term and immediate gains rather than investing in what it takes to nurture those gains.

The government continues to interfere with the pricing of agricultural outputs ostensibly to prevent exploitation of the poor by private traders. Yet, some actions by the same government fall short of addressing the vulnerability of the poor to exploitation by state officials and private traders. The government has quite often come in to stabilize prices of key crops, including the staple maize at harvest time without a corresponding reduction in the price for the basic farm input-fertilizer, except for the discriminatory input subsidy, only to raise the price later on when maize is scarce and at the time that the poor can hardly afford the commodity. The most negatively affected to date have been tobacco producers. Tobacco exports command a major share of Malawi's export revenue. For this reason tobacco is fondly termed 'green gold' to underscore its contribution to Malawi's economy. Unlike gold, tobacco is a commodity with extremely delicate market prospects and least reliable as a store of value for the peasant producers. Yet, and this is a nude fact, the luxury consumption of the political elite and urban based civil servants is bound up with the toil and sweat of the smallholder farmers and tenants who produce tobacco along with tradable amounts of food crops. It follows that net proceeds paradoxically accrue to the elite.

In recent years the marketing of tobacco has been characterized by disagreement over prices between tobacco sellers and buyers. The concern has been that tobacco buyers prosper, while the tobacco sellers remain poor due to low and unstable prices. The conventional explanation has been the trend may be attributed to the low quality of the leaf associated with high input prices especially of fertilizer prices that are well beyond the buying capacity of many smallholder farmers and the poor handling of the crop leading to presence of non-tobacco related materials (NTRM). However, global trends like growing competition from other tobacco producers; for instance increased tobacco production in neighbouring countries, in parts of South America and Asia (for instance in Brazil and China) and declining demand due to pressure from growing international anti-smoking lobby, suggest that tobacco farmers should not expect an improved supply of inputs and therefore better quality of tobacco to have any significant impact on stability of the price.

Low producer prices render farming non-competitive, generally unattractive and risky. Long term consequences are that national development efforts are compromised by fluctuations in the money value of exports. Malawi lacks control over national income or money supply and hence over its rate of development. The scenario of Malawi is not far from that of other southern African countries, what Morris (2000) calls international forces' rush to globalize markets, privatize land tenure and commercialize agriculture while paying scant attention to the needs and resources of the poor. Worse still, imperfections in the policy and market environment imply that relatively higher market prices enjoy received at the international market do not trickle down to the smallholder producers perpetually condemned to poverty by all sorts of direct and indirect taxation that sustain the appetites of or prop up corrupt and inefficient elites and civil servants (Mckay et al. 1997). Consequently, the tragedy of small-scale farmers is that they are exploited by two forces, one internal the other external; the 'international-market-forces' that also preys on soft and not freely convertible and peripheral currencies (Nyamnjoh 2000). This is true as Justinian Rweyemamu also observed: 'For what lies behind the veil of market forces is naked market power exercised through various measures adopted by the industrially powerful countries to increase their growth rates and exports – import quotas, intra-firm transactions, rigged markets' (Rweyemamu 1992).

Liberalization of currency

As macroeconomic imbalances continue to exert significant pressure on the economy, one of the notable indicators is shortage of foreign exchange which makes it difficult for the government and the private sector to operate at optimal levels. Devaluing the currency has been mentioned repeatedly as critical to addressing the shortage. It has been carried out sometimes with a sense of urgency as if devaluation is a foolproof means to prosperity.

In the early 1990s the dollar value of the Malawi Kwacha was US$ 0.25, and in the early 2000s it was US$ 0.008. At the present moment it is actually less than US$0.00141 implying that liberalization of exchange rate results in depreciation of the nominal exchange rate but also of the buying capacity. While a weak currency has been noted to improve international trade by making exports cheaper, the effects on the domestic market are far from rosy. The trend in Malawi is that the negative effects, for instance a rise in prices of all tradable goods erodes buying power of the poor; including the low salaried employees in urban and rural sectors; thus entrenching economic despondency. It is correct to argue that a nation cannot devalue its currency on its way to prosperity.

Following the devaluation of the Malawi Kwacha in August 1998 by over 30%, prices of all commodities including items produced locally went up by between 60 and 80% in nominal terms.[1] Traders hiked prices in anticipation of widespread inflation. They took advantage of the consumer confusion and government lukewarm commitment to consumer welfare. At the same time the price of fertilizer rose by over 60 %, triggering despair in the small-scale farming sector which ordinarily constitutes 75 % of the poor population. By compromising the majority of the population's access to essential commodities, liberalization of the currency compounds poverty and is a barrier to efforts by government, donors and individuals to eradicate poverty. This is true in a global context because globalization compounds the socio-economic situation by exposing poor population groups to profit maximizing greed of western corporations (Akokpari 2000) and of local business elite. The local business elite include if not just tied closely with the elite political interests; making market forces an imperfect yardstick for projecting socioeconomic welfare. Market ethic could be rationally impersonal but it is not blind to vested interests. Failure of the democratic promise and the rise and proliferation of clientele politics is a nude manifestation of the underlying anomalous political situation.

Pseudo-democratic promise and clientele politics

One of the characteristics of recent political reforms in Malawi is that political party officials, those from the ruling party in particular, carry along money from which they draw out cash handouts to reward praise singers. Good politics is defined as being generous and capable of providing some form of largess. Another form of patronage is political party clothing which is provided to supporters at political rallies, in work places and at funerals, sometimes on the premise of poverty alleviation. The trend started and was perfected in the late 1990s.[2] Then, as of now, what is astonishing is that the source of the money is undisclosed.[3] What is probably stunning is that amounts of money often handed out per capita are often meagre to make significant impact or reduce poverty. Besides perpetuating a culture of dependence, at the national level disguised as building development partnerships, the attractiveness of handouts just like dependence on foreign donations raise fundamental questions. Considering that the money given out is in small amounts, too little to have significant impact on poverty levels, it means that the benefactors are either ignorant of the scope and intensity of poverty or they are motivated by myopic elitism. It seems the motive of handouts is not poverty alleviation, as many recipients would confirm, rather a ploy to gain political mileage. This is also true with some foreign aid packages. Yet, the practice cripples initiative which any well-meaning leader would want to cultivate. It is tantamount to political corruption. The consolation is that eventually a growing number of people at the grassroots appreciate the costs of the culture of handouts. Misuse of public resources to support the culture of handouts is one diversionary tactic. Such a tactic is already responsible for the near total collapse of state companies, perennial drug shortages in health facilities, understaffing and overcrowding in schools and low funding levels in colleges and university campuses. There is also a growing awareness that generally corruption is undermining competitiveness central to a well-functioning market economy. It distorts the choice between activities and lowers returns to public as well as private investments. Low public spending on health and education limits opportunities for poor people to participate in economic life in the interim and in the long term as well.

Corruption is and will continue to weaken the legitimacy of the state (see World Bank 2002:106). Destruction of property of political and business elites and loss of life in the 20 July 2011 'nationwide' economic and governance demonstrations show that Malawians are fully aware and concerned with mismanagement going on in government and massive corruption of the proceeds from privatization and dislike petty arrogance of their political leaders. Such arrogance is compounded by the erroneous view that they could be above the law and that their private interests are equal to national interests.

It is disheartening that economic and political liberalizations have not nurtured transparency and accountability. Senior civil servants and political leaders in government, in parliament and even some members of the judiciary chose not to be accountable just as the agents and forces of economic globalization are in principle largely unaccountable (Mittleman 1995) to any group of citizens. These elites are responsible just as the unfavourable market conditions are for the plight of the poor. In the words of Ayi Kwei Armah: 'how long will Africa be cursed with its leaders' (Nyamnjoh 2000; Sandbrook 1982:77). Rising levels of corruption and the rhetoric to improve the condition of the poor are incongruent.

A brief account of some events in the last 20 years is quite instructive. The first president of Malawi had 'his' Press Holdings appropriated by the state when he left office in the 1990s for reasons that included personalization of investment initially made using public resources. His immediate successor was later accused of diverting foreign aid amounting to K1.7 billion (equivalent to US$12 million at the time) which was deposited into his personal bank account. Other claims against him included that he presided over the corrupt procurement of textbooks from a firm based in the United Kingdom and the Minister of Education at the time was sentenced to a prison term. Several of his ministers were further implicated in the misappropriation of K187 million in a classroom construction scandal. The family of his successor was embroiled in disagreement over his estate after his death. The state became entangled in a rather petty and bizarre fashion- from supporting the erstwhile widow, through dubious deceased estate duty valuation to state sponsored allegations of corrupt acquisition of wealth. Questionable disposal of real property belonging to the state has been a major challenge affecting various regimes. The climax was the mass looting of public coffers followed by effort to prolong the presidential term by some three months on the pretext of statesmanship and in order to correct electoral irregularities. Then a self-imposed exile followed just in time before it transpired that she was the chief architect of the looting of state resources known as 'cashgate'.

While corruption of the kind referred to above benefits the privileged, it hurts and deprives the poor of prospects of a better life. It raises ethical dilemmas. Preventing corruption and recovering stolen assets, stolen by the politically exposed persons (PEPs), are twin processes that can contribute to development.[4] The corollary is that the failure to curtail corruption and recover stolen assets essentially means denied development opportunities since the assets could be used to improve access to safe drinking water, primary health care, basic education, improved housing and security. Corruption is a hindrance to legitimate business. According to Akçay (2006) corruption reduces economic growth by retarding long-term domestic and foreign investments. It also enhances inflation, misallocates talent to rent seeking activities, pushes firms underground, distorts markets and the allocation of resources, increases income inequality and poverty, reduces tax revenues, distorts the fundamental role of the government (on enforcement of contracts and protection of property rights), and undermines the legitimacy of government and of the market economy (see also Jimu 2009, 2013). Recovery of stolen assets can go a long way in mitigating the harm that corruption causes and the effect that is has on rule of law, especially if perceived from the perspective that impunity can be overcome and therefore a virtuous circle can be initiated. Positive outcomes may include nurturing of good democratic governance and transparent leadership. Lack of development and irresponsible leadership can be principal obstacles to democracy and development.

Epilogue

Before 2011 it was obvious Malawi would be among countries in sub-Sahara Africa that were unlikely to halve poverty or achieve millennium development goals (MDGs) by 2015. The rationality of halving poverty rather than eradicating it altogether was baffling and controversial. For a country with over 50% of its population living in dire poverty, aiming at halving poverty implied taking half measures as practically it meant take half/leave half approach. Deciding whose poverty was to be eradicated must have involved difficult ethical questions for those who claim to be working for the just world. It sounds like some sort of conspiracy between the policy makers and financiers including the international development partners.

Theoretically after halving poverty there will be some more poverty for which new half if not quarter measures could be developed and implemented. The calculation implied should have been baffling. Pessimism is founded given the overall precarious socioeconomic situation. Perhaps it pays to be optimistic even though doing so may be sophistry. That the world halved poverty in the 20th century on other continents does not guarantee that the 21st century will be Africa's century, and perhaps Malawi's too. A brief overview of the statistics is needed to appreciate the dynamics.

The United Nations reported recently that globally the number of people living in extreme poverty declined by more than half, falling from 1.9 billion in 1990 to 836 million in 2015, with most progress occurring since 2000. Also, maternal mortality declined by 45% worldwide since 1990, with most of the reduction occurring since 2000. In Southern Asia, it declined by 64 per cent between 1990 and 2013, and in sub-Saharan Africa by 49 per cent. More generally there is admission that progress towards achieving MGDs had been uneven across regions and countries, leaving millions of people behind, especially the poorest and those disadvantaged due to sex, age, disability, ethnicity or geographic location.[5] The impact of raising the poverty line from US$ 1.25 to US$ 1.90 should be a reversal of gains claimed to date affecting a majority of those located just above the line.[6]

Sustainable development goals (SDGs) are good sounding as they stress everything from zero poverty, zero hunger, good health, quality education, gender equality, clean water and sanitation, and affordable clean energy, to decent work and economic growth, innovation, reduced inequalities, sustainable cities, responsible consumption, climate action, unpolluted oceans and land, and partnerships.[7] Just like with MGDs, it is too early for Malawi and other developing and peripheral nations to rejoice.

Malawi's apparent dismal development can best be approached and understood by disentangling specific contradictions and the logic of the world expansion of capitalism. For the internal contradictions, the weak economic base, work ethics, maladministration and corruption, lackadaisical approach to rule of law, accountability and good governance are some of the major challenges. The problems of low levels of development funding, low productivity, low returns on investment and more specifically of corruption cannot be solved effectively when the head of state is an accomplice in the looting of public coffers. It cannot be achieved when his or her spouse, offspring, siblings, in-laws, and political party campaign directors are involved and public resources are being siphoned for the purpose of advancing the ruling party agenda, to bolster the re-election prospects of the incumbent head of state or that of their anointed successor. And when elected they fail to draw up a line between what belongs to state from that which is their own. Worse still if they fail to canvass for national consensus, mobilize domestic resources and institute strategies that could motivate improved productivity, international competitiveness and income distribution.

Sometimes a fix is not easy to come by because of the syndrome of recycled leaders. Paul Baran writing On *the Political Economy of Backwardness* cautioned that the keepers of the past cannot be the builders of the future. Although Baran advanced the argument more as a critic of dependency and the tendency to look west for solutions to problems of development, it applies literary also to the practice of recycling leaders since it effectively means recycling ideals and ideas that have not and perhaps would not work at all. Unfortunately, change of leadership has sometimes meant loss of direction when visionary and technically competent persons have been replaced with mediocre populist.

There is urgent need to create and sustain institutions that mobilize and conscientise the poor and the rich rather than perpetuating political structures that serve as instruments of manipulation. The unfortunate outcome is perpetuation of politics of poverty and elite hold on power (Nyamnjoh 2000). Quality leadership, leadership that is focused and motivated by desire to uplift socioeconomic development is a necessary condition for poverty reduction and sustainable development effort. Poverty of leadership manifests itself in a myriad of ways such as lack of fairer appreciation of needs and priority areas, inimical foreign agenda, pursuit of futile and inappropriate plans, gross mediocrity and inconsiderate and shameless acts of corruption, tribalism, nepotism, impunity, extravagance, arrogance, indiscretion and disregard of good counsel. With such a brand of leadership it is inconceivable that a nation can halve or eradicate poverty. Rather, the plight of the poorest receives less attention while the leader is busy feasting, jostling and jockeying for power, wealth and influence in a country overburdened by indebtedness, hunger and acute shortage of essential drugs, skyrocketing prices and foreign exchange deficits, hopeless staffing levels in critical sectors such as education, agriculture, health and security. Where these aspects are defining conditions the challenge is not that political leaders are lacking, it is rather that good leaders are few, misplaced, starved of opportunity or pre-empted by opportunists and opportunism.

Frank Stilwell alerts us that this trend of affairs is to be expected where economic self-interests and rent seeking permeate social order and political processes (Stilwell 2002). The major challenge is not the lack of ideology but of pragmatic approach to enduring challenges including those to do with resource constraints and also challenges posed by globalization and widening disparities in the distribution of wealth. With respect to resource constraints, Mussa and Pauw

(2011) draw our attention to the challenge of high fertility rate and the significant relationship it has to poverty eradication. Poor households in general tend to be larger than non-poor ones and have higher dependency ratios. Also, household heads in poor households typically have little or no education, and for this reason have a lower likelihood of being in salaried employment or of working in a household enterprise. These relationships are an invitation to serious reflection to the challenge of addressing high fertility rates and the dangers of an ever-growing population. These include complications associated with feeding, housing, and caring for a large section of non-working and non-productive population.

Finally, there is a need to depoliticize development. Depoliticizing development is actually one of the contentious issues, especially in light of strong temptation among politicians to prolong their hold on power legitimately and illegitimately and to exploit state resources and institutions towards rewarding friends and supporters on the one hand and to punish those considered enemies on the other hand. Fairness in the distribution of national wealth and development is yet another requirement in the interest of promoting development and national unity. Nothing can be close to fairness where laws, policies and regulations on public order and security, trade, access to food, health and education, foreign exchange control, anti-corruption and taxation are used to punish or silence critics and 'enemies', through and by among other measures overregulated and denied access, repeated investigations, audits and arrests. These are counterproductive since they cannot lead to more food, better health, higher income per capita, better education and more gainful employment opportunities, better amenities, greater security and healthier, happier and long life for all. Integrity, responsibility, respect for rule of law and order, love of work, effort to save and invest and efficiency are important virtues worth upholding and consolidating.

Notes

[1] See 4th quarter edition of the Economist Intelligence Unit, 1998 Country Report for Malawi.

[2] The president would give a donation of K50, 000 to journalists and civil society leaders who make themselves available for media interface or consultative meetings. Some recipients have in the past decided to play Good Samaritan by donating the cash handouts to various causes. The morality of giving, receiving and donating is obviously a contentious matter.

[3] Economic Intelligence Unit, 1998 (the 4th Quarter edition) for an earlier critique of the practice.

[4] Studies on the challenges of corruption and benefits of recovering stolen wealth (Jimu 2009, 2013) have shown that every US$100 million lost or recovered could fund first-line treatment for over 600,000 people with HIV/AIDS for a full year; or between 50 and 100 million people in drugs for the treatment of malaria; or provide 250,000 water connections for poor households, or finance full immunizations for 4 million children. The World Bank and United Nations office on drugs and crime *Fact Sheet on Stolen Asset Recovery* http://www.unodc.org/pdf/Star_FactSheet.pdf , or Asset Recovery - A Breakthrough by the UN Convention against Corruption (UNCAC) http://www.gtz.de/de/doumente/en-gtz-asset-recovery-2007.pdf

[5] http://www.un.org/apps/news/story.asp?NewsID=52922#.Vp06mLFBt UE (accessed on 18 January 2016).

[6] It sounds like moving goal posts and in deed this has been the trend. In 1985 the line was set at US$ 1.00/day. It was revised in 1993 to $1.08/day, then in 2005 to US$1.25 and recently in 2015 to US$1.90. It is

claimed that the change in the poverty line does not have any effect in real terms. See article submitted by Francisco Ferreira el al (2015) 'The international poverty line has just been raised to $1.90 a day, but global poverty is basically unchanged. How is that even possible?', http://blogs.worldbank.org/developmenttalk/international-poverty-line-has-just-been-raised-190-day-global-poverty-basically-unchanged-how-even (accessed on 18 January, 2016).

[7] See United Nations News Centre: http://www.un.org/apps/news/story.asp?NewsID=52922#.Vp06mLFBr UE (accessed 18 January, 2016).

228

References

African Development Bank (1995) *African Development Report*. New York: Oxford University Press.

Akçay, S. (2006) *Corruption and Human Development*, 26 CATO J. 29, 29-30. http://www.cato.org/pubs/journal/cj26n1/cj26n1-2.pdf

Akokpari J.K. (2000) 'Globalization and migration in Africa', *African Sociological Review*, 4 (2) 72 – 92.

Alexander, J. and Alexander, P. (1995) 'Commodification and consumption in a central Borneo community', *Koninklijk Instituut Voor Taal-, Land-en Volkenkunde*, 151 (II), 179 – 193.

Allman, J. (1996) 'Rounding up spinsters: gender chaos and unmarried women in colonial Asante', *Journal of African History* 37, 195 – 214.

Appadurai, A. (1986) 'Introduction: Commodities and the politics of value', in A. Appadurai (ed.) *The Social Life of Thing: commodities in cultural perspective*, pp. 3 – 63. Cambridge: Cambridge University Press.

Appendini, K. (2001), 'Land and livelihood: What do we know, and what are the issues?' In: A. Zoomers (ed.), *Land and Sustainable Livelihood in Latin America*, Amsterdam: Royal Tropical Institute/Vervuert Verlag, pp. 23 – 38.

Araujo, C. (2003) 'Non-agricultural employment growth and rural poverty reduction in Mexico during the 90s', Department of Agricultural and Resource Economics,

University of California, Berkeley. http://are.berkeley.edu/~araujo/Paper3-araujo.pdf

Balshaw, M. and Kennedy, L. (2000) 'Introduction: Urban space and representation' in Balshaw, M. and Kennedy L. (eds.), *Urban Space Representation*, London: Pluto.

Bandarage, A. (1984), 'Women in development: liberalism, Marxism and Marxism-feminism' in *Development and Change,* Vol. 15 pp 495-515. London: sage

Bardhan, P. (1984) *The Political Economy of Development in India.* Oxford and New York: Basil Blackwell

Barker, J. (1984) 'Politics and production', in Barker, J. (ed.) *The Politics of Agriculture in Tropical Africa.* Beverly Hills, California: Sage Publications. Pp 11-34.

Barnett, T. (1988) *Sociology and Development.* Hutchinson Education/Routledge

Bayat, A. (1997) *Street Politics: poor people's movements in Iran,* New York: Columbia University Press.

de Beauvoir, S. (1949) *The Second Sex.* David Campbell Publishers Ltd. (Translated by Jonathan Cape (1953)

Bebbington, A. (1999), 'Capitals and capabilities: A framework for analysing peasant

viability, rural livelihoods and poverty', *World Development* 27 (12): 2021 – 44.

Benediktsson, K. (2002) *Harvesting Development: the construction of fresh food markets in Papua New Guinea.* Ann Arbor: The University of Michigan Press.

Bernstein, H. (1996), 'Agrarian questions then and now', in Bernstein, H. and Brass, T. (eds.), *Agrarian Questions*, London: Frank Cass.

Bernstein, H. (1992a), Introduction: Rural livelihoods: crises and responses, in Bernstein, H., Crow, H and Johnson, H, (eds.) *Rural Livelihoods: Crises and responses*, Oxford: Oxford University Press in association with the Open University, Milton Keynes.

Bernstein, H. (1992b), 'Poverty and the poor' in Bernstein, H., Crow, H and Johnson, H, (eds.) *Rural Livelihoods: Crises and responses*, Oxford: Oxford University Press in association with the Open University, Milton Keynes.

Bernstein, H. (1992c), 'Agrarian structures and change: Latin America', in Bernstein, H., Crow, H and Johnson, H, (eds.) *Rural Livelihoods: Crises and responses*, Oxford: Oxford University Press in association with the Open University, Milton Keynes.

Bernstein, H. (1992d), 'Agrarian structures and change: Sub-Saharan Africa', in Bernstein, H., Crow, H and Johnson, H, (eds.) *Rural Livelihoods: Crises and responses*, Oxford: Oxford University Press in association with the Open University, Milton Keynes.

Berry, S. (1984) 'The food crisis and agrarian change in Africa: A review essay', *African Studies Review*, 27 (2):59 – 112.

Bienefeld, M. (1986) 'Analyzing the politics of African state policy: some thought on Robert Bate's work', in *IDS Bulletin*, 21 (1).

Blantyre City Assembly (2000) *Urban Structure Plan Vol. III*. Blantyre.

Blantyre District Assembly (2007) *Blantyre Rural District Education Plan, 2008/2009 – 2010/2011*. Blantyre District.

Bohannan, P and Bohannan, L. (1968) *Tiv Economy*, Evanston: Northwestern University Press.

Boserup, E. (1970) *Women's Role in economic Development.* New York: St Martins Press.

Braig, M. (2000) 'Women's interests in development theory and policy, from WID to 'mainstreaming gender' in *Development and Cooperation* No. 2: 13 – 16.

Bromley, R.D.F. (1998) 'Informal commerce: expansion and exclusion in the historical center of the Latin American city', *International Journal of Urban and Regional Research,* 22 (2): 245 – 264.

Bryceson, D.F. (1995) 'African women hoe cultivators: speculative origins and current enigmas, in Bryceson, D.F. (ed.) *Women Wielding the Hoe. Lessons from rural Africa for Feminist Theory and development practice.* Oxford: Berg Publishers. Pp 3 – 22.

Bryceson, D.F. (1999) 'African rural labour, income diversification & livelihood approaches: a long-term development perspective', *Review of African Political Economy,* Vol. 26 (80): 171 – 189.

Buchanan, J (1885) The Shire Highlands: As colony and mission, London: William Blackwood and Sons.

Buell, R.L. (1965) *The Native Problem in Africa.* London: Frank Cass & Co. Ltd. (Second impression) First edition published in 1928 by The Bureau of International Research of Harvard University.

Burkey, S. (1993) *People First: a guide to self-reliant participatory rural development,* London: Zed Books Ltd.

Campbell, B. (1994) Praise the community, blame the mothers, *The Independent* 30 – 11 – 1994.

Cannon, T. and Smith, D. (2002) 'Rural Non-Farm Economy Project: Uganda Fieldwork Case Study Synthesis Report'. Natural Resource Institute NRI Report No. 2701

Carr, M. (ed) (1991) *Women and food Security: The experiences of the SADC Countries.* London: Intermediate Technology Publications.

Carswell, G. (2002) Livelihood diversification: increasing in importance or increasingly recognized? evidence from southern Ethiopia, *Journal of International Development* 14: 789-804.

Centre for Policy Dialogue (CPD) (2004), 'Promoting rural non-farm economy: Is Bangladesh Doing Enough?' Report No. 66.
http://unpan1.un.org/intradoc/groups/public/documents/APCITY/UNPAN018962.pdf

Chambers, R. and Conway, G.R. (1992) *Sustainable Rural Livelihoods: Practical concepts for the 21st century.* Brighton: Institute of Development Studies.

Chambers, R. (1989) 'Vulnerability, Coping and Policy', *Institute of Development Studies Bulletin,* 20 (2): 1 – 7.

Chambers, R. (1983), *Rural Development: putting the last first,* London: Longman.

Chirwa, E.W. Kydd, J and Dorward, A (2006) Future Scenarios for Agriculture in Malawi: Challenges and Dilemmas, Paper to be presented at the *Future Agricultures Consortium* held at the Institute of Development Studies, Sussex, 20 – 21 March 2006.)

Chirwa, E.W. (2007) 'Targeting and Exclusion Experiences in Public Works Programmes in Malawi' Regional Hunger

and Vulnerability Programme Regional Evidence Building Agenda (REBA).
http://www.wahenga.net/uploads/documents/reports/REBA%20-%20Malawi%20-%20Public%20Works%20Programmes.pdf

Chirwa, W. (1997) 'The Garden of Eden': Sharecropping on the Shire Highlands Estates, 1920-1945, in Jeeves, A.H. and Crush, J. (eds) (1997) *White Farms, Black Labour: The state and agrarian change in southern Africa, 1910 – 1950.* Portsmouth, NH: Heinemann.

Cleaver, K.M. and Donovan, W.G. (1994) 'Agriculture, poverty, and policy reform in sub-Saharan Africa' World Bank Discussion papers No. 280, African Technical Department Series.

Cleaver, F. (1994), 'Managing participation: the case of rural water supply', in Analoui, F. (ed.), *The Realities of Managing Development Projects.* Aldershot: Averbury.

Cromwell, E. (1996) *Governments, Farmers and Seeds in a Changing Africa.* Oxon: CBA International.

Cross, J.C. (1998) *Informal Politics: Street Vendors and the state in Mexico,* Stanford, California: Stanford University Press.

Davis, J.R and Bezemer, D.J. (2004) *The Development of Non-Farm Economy in Developing Countries and Transition Economies: Key Emerging and Conceptual Issues.* Chatham, UK: Natural Resources Institute
http://www.nri.org/projects/rnfe/pub/papers/keyissues.pdf

Dear, M. (1997), 'Postmoderm Bloodliness', in Benko, G. and Strohmayer, U. (eds.),

Space and Social Theory: interpreting modernity and postmodernity, Oxford: Blackwell, pp 49-71.

Delgado, C.D. and Siamwalla, A. (1997) 'Rural Economy and Farm Income Diversification in Developing Countries', Paper presented at a Plenary Session of the XXIII International Conference of Agricultural Economists, Sacramento, CA, U.S.A., August 10-16, 1997. MSSD DISCUSSION PAPER NO. 20 International Food Policy Research Institute Washington DC, 20036 USA

Department for International Development (2007) *Malawi Country Governance Analysis* http://www.dfid.gov.uk/consultations/malawicga.pdf

Dercon S and Krishnan P (1996) 'Income Portfolio in Rural Ethiopia and Tanzania: Choices and Constraints', *Journal of Development Studies*, 32 (6), 850 – 75.

Desai, V. and Potter, R.B. (eds.) (2008) *The Companion to Development Studies* (2nd edition). London: Hodder Education.

Dixon, C. (1990) *Rural Development in the Third World*, New York: Routledge.

Dorward, A., Guenther, B., Wheeler, R. S. (2008) 'Linking social protection and support to small farmer development: Malawi Case Study', A paper commissioned by FAO. http://www.fao.org/es/esa/pdf/workshop_0108_malawi.pdf (accessed 14 March 2009)

Douglas, J. (2000) 'Malawi: Blantyre & Lilongwe' Travel *Africa* 13th edition, Autumn. Available at http://www.travelafricamag.com/index2.php?option=com_content&do_pdf=1&id=345

Duflo, E. and Udry, C (2003) 'Intrahousehold Resource Allocation in Cote d'Ivoire: Social Norms, Separate Accounts and Consumption Choices'
http://econ-www.mit.edu/files/764

Economist Intelligence Unit (EIU) (1998) *Country Report, Malawi* 3rd Quarter

Economist Intelligence Unit (EIU) (1998) *Country Report, Malawi* 4th Quarter

Eicher, C.K. and Baker, D.C. (1982), *Research on agricultural development in sub-Saharan Africa: A critical Survey*, Michigan: Michigan State University.

Ellis, F. (1988) *Peasant economics: Farm households and agrarian development*, Cambridge: Cambridge University Press.

Ellis, F. (1999) 'Rural livelihood diversity in developing countries: evidence and policy implications', Overseas Development Institute, Number 40. http://www.odi.org.uk/resources/specialist/natural-resource-perspectives/40-rural-livelihood-diversity.pdf

Ellis, F. (2005, June) 'Small-farms, livelihood diversification and rural urban transitions: strategic Issues in sub-Saharan Africa', Read at a conference on *The Future of Small Farms Organized,* International Food Policy Research Institute (IFPRI), Imperial College, Wye, Kent, UK. http://www.ifpri.org/events/seminars/2005/smallfarms/ellis.pdf

Ellis, F. and Freeman, A. (2002) 'Rural Livelihoods and Poverty Reduction Strategies in Four African Countries' LADDER Working Paper no. 30. Overseas Development Group (ODP), University of East Anglia, Norwich NR4

7TJ, UK; and ICRISAT, United nations Avenue, Nairobi, Kenya.

Englund, H. (1999) 'The self in self-interest: Land, labour and temporalities in Malawi's agrarian change', Africa, 69, 1.

Englund, H. (2000) 'The dead hand of human rights: contrasting Christianities in post-transition Malawi', *The Journal of Modern African Studies*, 38, 4, pp 579-603.

Englund, H. (2002) 'The village in the city, the city in the village: migrants in Lilongwe', *Journal of Southern African Studies*, vol. 28 (1), pp 137-154.

Escobar, J. (2001) 'Determinants of non-farm income diversification in rural Peru', *The Journal of Development Studies,* 29 (3), pp 497 – 508

Feder, E. (1976) 'McNamara's Little Green Revolution, World Bank Scheme for Self-Liquidation of Third World peasantry' in *Economic and Political Weekly*, April 3, 1976.

Ferguson, A.E. (1994) Gendered Science: A Critique of Agricultural Development, *American Anthropologist* 96, (3), pp. 540 – 552.

Fidzani, N.H, Makepe, P. and Tlhalefang, J. (1996), 'The impact of trade liberalization on Botswana's beef and maize sectors', Prepared for Botswana Institute for Development Policy Analysis (BIDPA).

Francis, E. and Murray, C. (2002) Special Issue on Changing Livelihoods: Introduction, *Journal of Southern African Studies*, Vol. 28, No. 3, Special Issue: Changing Livelihoods (Sep., 2002), pp. 485-487

Francis, P. et al. (1996), *State, Community and Local Development in Nigeria*, Washington DC: World Bank.

Frank, A.G. (1992), 'The development of underdevelopment', in Wilber, C. and Jameson, K. (eds.), *The Political Economy of Development and Underdevelopment,* New York: McGraw

Foster-Carter, A. (1985), *The Sociology of Development.* Lancashire: Causeway.

Geertz, C. (1963) *Agricultural Involution: the Process of Ecological Change in Indonesia.* Berkeley, CA: University of California Press.

Gluckman, M. (ed.) (1969) *Ideas and Procedures in African Customary Law.* London: Oxford University Press.

Goheen, M. (1992) 'Chiefs, sub-chiefs and local control: negotiations over land, struggles over meaning', *Africa* 63 (3), 389 – 412.

González, M.C. (2003) 'An ethics for postcolonial ethnography', in R.P Clair (ed) *Expressions of Ethnography: novel approaches to qualitative methods,* pp. 77 – 86. Albany: State University of New York.

Government of Botswana (1991) *National Development Plan 7, 1991- 2007.* Gaborone: Ministry of Finance and Development Planning.

Government of Botswana (1997) *National Development Plan 8, 1997/8 – 2002/3.* Gaborone: Ministry of Finance and Development Planning.

Government of Malawi (1995) *Policy Framework for Poverty Alleviation Programmes.* Ministry of Economic Planning and Development.

Government of Malawi (2000) 'The State of Malawi's Poor: The incidence, depth, and severity of poverty.' Poverty Monitoring Systems (PMS) briefing No. 2 (revised). Zomba:

National Statistical Office.

Government of Malawi (2001) *A Relative Profile of Poverty in Malawi, 1998: A quintile-based poverty analysis of the Malawi Integrated Household Survey, 1997-98*, NSO and National Economic Council

Government of Malawi (2005) *Household Socio-economic Characteristics, Integrated Household Survey 2004/05*, Zomba: National Statistics Office.

Government of Malawi (2008) *2008 Population and Housing Census: Preliminary report*, Zomba: National Statistical Office.

Government of Malawi (2009) *Population and Housing Census 2008: Main Report*. Zomba: National Statistical Office.

Government of Malawi (2010) *Malawi State of Environment and Outlook Report: Environment for Sustainable Economic Growth*. Lilongwe: Ministry if Natural Resources, Energy and Environment.

Government of Malawi and National Statistics Office (2012) *Gender and Development Index 2011*. Lilongwe: Ministry of Gender, Children and Community Development and National Statistical Office

Gregory C.A. and Altman J.C. (1989) *Observing the Economy*, London: Routledge.

Guyer, J. (1980) 'Food, cocoa, and the division of labour by sex in two West African societies.' *Comparative Studies in Society and History* 22(3), 355—373

Guyer, J.L. (1986) 'Intra-household processes and farming systems research: perspectives from Anthropology', in Moock, J.L. (ed) *Understanding Africa's Rural Households and Farming Systems*. Boulder, Colorado: Westview Press, Inc. pp 92-104.

de Haan, L., and Zoomers, A. (2005) 'Exploring the frontier of livelihoods research', *Development and Change* 36(1):27–47.

de Haan, L.J. (2010) 'Perspectives on African studies and development in sub-Saharan Africa', *Africa Spectrum* 45 (1), 95-116.

Haddad, L. and Hoddinott, J. (1994) 'Women's income and boy girl anthropometric status in the Cote d'Ivoire.' *World Development* 18(2), 197—214

Harrigan, J. (2001) *From Dictatorship to Democracy: Economic policy in Malawi 1964-2000,* Aldershot: Ashgate Publishing Ltd.

Harris, J. (1982) *Rural Development: theories of peasant economy and agrarian change.* London: Hutchinson (Publishers) Ltd.

Harrison, D. (1996). 'Sustainability and tourism: Reflections from a muddy pool', in Archer, B. Briguglio, L. Jafari, J. and Wall, G. (eds.) *Sustainable Tourism in Island and Small States, Vol. I, Theoretical issues* (pp. 69-89). London: Mansell.

Hart, K. (1973), 'Informal income opportunities and urban employment in Ghana', in *The Journal of African Studies, 11 (1), Pp 61-89.*

Hart, K. (2006) 'Informal Economy' 18 December 2006 Filed under: The African Revolution, Economy — keith @ 10:34 am

http://www.thememorybank.co.uk/2006/12/18/informal-economy/#more-106 (last accessed on 12 February 2008)

Hart, K. (2007) 'The Urban Informal Economy in Retrospect' 8 June 2007, Filed under: Economy — keith @ 8:38 pm http://www.thememorybank.co.uk/2007/06/08/the-urban-informal-eocnomy-in-retrospect/ (accessed on 14 February 2008)

Hesselberg, Jan (1985), *The Third World in Transition: the case of the peasantry in Botswana*, Scandinavian Institute of African Studies, Uppsala.

Himmelstrand, U. (1994) 'Perspectives, Controversies and Dilemmas in the Study of African Development' in Himmelstrand, U., Kinyanjui, K. and Mburugu, E. *African Perspectives on Development: Controversies, dilemmas and openings.* Nairobi: East African Education Publishers.

Hirschmann, D. and Vaughan, M. (1983) 'Food production and income generation in a matrilineal society: rural women in Zomba, Malawi', Journal *of Southern African Studies*, Vol. 10, No. 1, October 1983. Pp. 86-99.

Hull, R.W. (1980) *Modern Africa: Change and continuity*, Englewood Cliffs, N.J.: Prentice-Hall, Inc.

Hussein, K and Nelson, J. (1998) 'Sustainable Livelihoods and Livelihood Diversification'. IDS Working Paper 69.

Hyden, G. (1986) 'The invisible economy of smallholder agriculture in Africa', in Moock, J.L. (ed) *Understanding Africa's Rural Households and Farming Systems.* Boulder, Colorado: Westview Press, Inc. pp 11-35.

James, D. (2007) *Gaining Ground: 'rights' and 'property' in South African land reform.* Oxon and New York: Routledge.

Jimu, I.M. (2003) 'Appropriation and Mediation of Urban Spaces: Growth, dynamics and politics of street vending in Blantyre, Malawi' Unpublished MA Thesis, School of Graduate Studies (Department of Sociology), University of Botswana.

Jimu, I.M. (2005) 'Negotiated economic opportunity and power: Perceptions and perspectives of street vending in Malawi' *Africa Development* XXX, No. 4, 2005, pp. 35-51.

Jimu, I. M. (2008a) *Urban Appropriation and Transformation: Bicycle taxi and handcart operators in Mzuzu, Malawi.* Menkon, Bamenda (Cameroon): Langaa Research & Publishing CIG.

Jimu, I.M. (2008b) 'Community Development: a cross examination of theory and practice using experiences in rural Malawi', Africa *Development* 33 (2), 23 – 35.

Jimu I.M. (2009) 'Managing Proceeds of Asset Recovery: The case of Nigeria, Peru, the Philippines and Kazakhstan', Working Paper No. 6, Working Paper Series, International Centre for Asset Recovery, Basel Institute on Governance (Switzerland).

Jimu, I.M. (2011) 'Peri-urban Land Transactions: Everyday practices and relations in peri-urban Blantyre, Malawi', PhD Thesis, Institute of Social Anthropology, University of Basel, Switzerland.

Jimu, I.M. (2012) *Peri-urban Land Transactions: Everyday practices and relations in peri-urban Blantyre, Malawi.* Bamenda: Langaa

Jimu, I.M. (2013) 'Asset recovery and the civil society in perspective: Nigeria, Peru, the Philippines and Kazakhstan cases considered', in Zinkernagel, G.F., Monteith, C. and Pereira, P.G. (eds) *Emerging Trends in Asset Recovery.* Bern: Peter Lang/ Basel Institute on Governance. pp. 317 – 328.

Jones, W.O. (1960) 'Economic man in Africa', *Food Research Institute Studies*, pp. 107 – 134.

Jones, H (1990) *Population Geography.* London: Paul Chapman Publishing Ltd.

Kabra, K. N, (2005), 'Rural Industrialisation in China: A Saga of Township and Village Enterprises, 1978-2002', in

Rohini Nayyar and Alak N. Sharma (eds.), op. cit., pp.35-48.

Kadzandira, J.M. (2007) 'A Study of Recipient and Community Experience of the Delivery of the Malawi Input Subsidy Programme 2006/07', http://www.wahenga.net/uploads/documents/reports/REBA%20-%20Malawi%20-%20Input%20Subsidy%20Programme.pdf

Kaitilla, S. (1999) 'Invisible real estate agents and urban housing development on customary land in Papua New Guinea', *Environment and Urbanization* 11 (1), 267 – 276

Kandawire, J.A.K. (1977) 'Thangata in pre-colonial and colonial systems of land tenure in southern Malawi with special reference to Chingale', *Africa* 47 (2), 185 – 191.

Kaufman, M. (1997a) 'Community power, grassroots democracy, and the transformation of social life', in Kaufman, M. and Alfonso, H.D. (eds.), *Community Power and Grassroots Democracy: the transformation of social life*, London: Zed Books.

Kaufman, M. (1997b), 'Differential participation: men, women and popular power', in Kaufman, M. and Alfonso, H.D. (eds.), *Community Power and Grassroots Democracy: the transformation of social life*, London: Zed Books

Kenyatta, J. (1971) *Facing Mount Kenya: the tribal life of the Gikuyu* (fifth impression). London: Secker & Warburg. (First published in 1938).

Kerski, J. and Ross, S. (2005) *The Essentials of the Environment*. Hodder Arnold.

Khaila, S.W., Mvula, P.M. and Kadzandira, J.M. (1999) Consultation with the Poor: Country synthesis, Malawi.

Report submitted to The Poverty Group, Poverty Reduction and Economic Management Network, World Bank Washington, D.C

Kulemeka, P. (2000) 'The Malawi Case Study' Inter-Agency Forum (FAO, DFID, UNDP, WFP, IFAD): *Operationalising Participatory Ways of Applying Sustainable Livelihoods Approaches Siena*, March 7 – 11, 2000 http://www.onefish.org/cds_upload/1300.Malawi_case_stud y_.2001-5-6.PDF

Laguerre, M.S. (1994) *The Informal City*, London: MacMillan.

Lawson, S. (1997) 'The tyranny of tradition: critical reflections on nationalist narratives in the South Pacific' in N. Thomas and T. Otto (eds) *Narratives of Nation in the South* Pacific pp. 15 – 31. Amsterdam: Harwood Academic Publishers.

Lawson, M., Cullen, A., Sibale, B., Ligomeka, S. and Lwanda, F. (2001) *Targeted Inputs Programme (TIP): Findings of the Monitoring Component for TIP 2000- 2001*. A monitoring study commissioned for the Ministry of Agriculture and Irrigation of the Government of Malawi by the U.K. Department for International Development. Available on: http://www.rdg.ac.uk/ssc/workareas/development/mala wi/tip1mon.pdf

Lentz, C. (2007) 'Land and the politics of belonging in Africa', in P. Chabal, U. Engel and L. de Haan (eds) *African Alternatives*, pp. 37 – 58. Leiden: Brill.

Liedholm, C., McPherson, M. and Chuta, E., (1994) 'Small enterprise employment growth in rural Africa', *American Journal of Agricultural Economics*, 76 (Dec.): 1177-1182.

Lindskog, P.A. (1982) 'The historical development of market-places and changes in their spatio-temporal integration in

Malaŵi', *Geografiska Annaler. Series B, Human Geography*, 64 (1): 61 – 67.

Lipton, M. (1974), 'Towards a theory of land reform' in Lehmann, D. (ed), *Agrarian Reform and Agrarian Reformism: studies of Peru, Chile, China and India*. London: Faber and Faber

Low, A. (1986), *Agricultural Development in Southern Africa: farm household economic and the food crisis*. London: James Currey.

Lowe, R.G. (1986), *Agricultural revolution in Africa: impediments to change and implications for farming, for education and for society*. London: Macmillan.

Lrz, X., Lin, L., Thirtle, C. and Wiggins, S. (2001) 'Agricultural Productivity Growth and Poverty Alleviation', *Development Policy Review*, vol. 19, no. 4, pp. 449 - 466.

Luke, T.W. (1995) 'Sustainable development as a power/knowledge system: The problem of 'governmentality', in Fischer, F. and Black, M. (eds.) *Greening environmental policy: The politics of a sustainable future* (pp. 3-20). New York: St Martins Press.

Mafeje, A. (1992) 'Is rural development possible in Africa?: a commentary on some sociological and historical blind-spots' CODESRIA Bulletin (4).

Malawi Economic Justice Network (MEJN) *Civil Society Budget Monitoring 2002/2003*.

Malawi Economic Justice Network (MEJN) 'How Priority Poverty Expenditures are Implemented' Civil Society Agriculture Network (CISANET) Civil Society Budget Monitoring 2002/2003.

Mallorie, E. (2003) 'The Role of women in agriculture and related rural livelihoods' CARE SDU Reports and Studies, CARE   Bangladesh. http://www.carebd.org/publication.pdf

Mandala, E. (1984) 'Capitalism, Kinship and Gender in the Lower Tchiri (Shire) Valley of Malawi, 1960-1960: An alternative theoretical framework'. *Africa Economic History* No. 13 pp 137-169.

Mann, K. (2007) *Slavery and the Birth of an African City: Lagos, 1760 – 1900.* Bloomington and Indianapolis: Indiana University Press.

Manona, C. (2001) 'De-agrarianization and rural-urban interactions' in Coetzee, J., Graaff, J., Hendricks, F. and Wood, G (eds.) *Development Theory Policy and Practice.* Cape Town: Oxford University Press Southern Africa.

Marschke, M. J., and F. Berkes (2006) 'Exploring strategies that build livelihood resilience: a case from Cambodia'. *Ecology and Society* 11(1): 42. [online] URL: http://www.ecologyandsociety.org/vol11/iss1/art42/

Mathur, H.M. (1986), *Administering Development in the Third World: constraints and choices*, New Delhi: Sage publications.

Mayer, E. (2002) *The Articulated Peasant: Household economics in the Andes*, Boulder, Colorado: Westview Press.

Mckay D., Morrissey, O. and Vaillant, C. (1997) 'Trade liberalization and agricultural supply responses: issues and lessons', *The European Journal of Development Research* Vol. 9 (2) pp. 129-147.

McCracken, J. (1968) 'The nineteenth century in Malawi', in T.O. Ranger (ed) *Aspects of Central African History*, pp 97 – 111. London: Heinemann Educational Books Ltd.

Meillassoux, C. (1965) *Anthropologie Economique des Gouros de Cote d'Ivoire* (Paris: F. Maspero)

Minde, I.J. and T.O. Nakhumwa (1998) 'Unrecorded cross-Border trade Between Malawi and neighboring Countries'. Technical Paper No. 90- Productive Sector Growth and Environment Office of sustainable Development Bureau for Africa. USAID.

Mitchell, J.C. (1968) 'The Yao of southern Nyasaland', in E. Colson and M. Gluckman (eds.) *Seven Tribes of Central Africa,* pp. 292 – 353. Manchester University Press.

Mittleman, J.M. (1995) 'Rethinking the International Division of Labour in the Context of Globalisation', *Third World Quarterly* Vol.16 (2) 273

Mohammed, O. (1989) Beekeeping in a Gambian village, *Community Development Journal An International Forum,* Vol. 24 (4), pp 240-246.

Momsen, J.H. (1991), *Women and development in the Third World,* London: Routledge.

Morris, S. (2000) 'Clientelism, corruption and catastrophe', *Review of African Political Economy* No 85. Pp 427 – 444.

Morrissey, O. and Filatotchev, D. (2000) 'Globalization and trade: the implications for exports from marginalized economies', *The Journal of Development Studies* Vol.37 (2) pp 1-12

Moyo, S. (2010) 'The Zimbabwe crisis, land reform and normalisation', in W. Anseeuw and C. Alden (eds) *The Struggle Over Land in Africa: conflicts, politics & change,* pp 245 – 264. Cape Town: HSRC Press.

Msilimba, G.C.G. (2007) 'A Comparative Study of Landslides and Geohazard Mitigation in Northern and Central

Malawi', Unpublished PhD Thesis, Faculty of Agricultural and Natural Sciences, Department of Geography, University of the Free State.

Murry, A.J. (1991) *No Money, No Honey: A study of street traders and prostitutes in Jakarta*, Singapore: Oxford University Press.

Murty, C.S. (2005) 'Rural Non-agricultural Employment in India: The Residual Sector Hypothesis Revisited', Centre for Economic and Social Studies Working Paper No. 67 Begumpet, Hyderabad-500016

Mussa, R. and Pauw, K. (2011) 'Poverty in Malawi: Current status and knowledge gap', Malawi Support Strategy Program (MaSSP) Policy Note 9, December 2011.

International Food Policy Research Institute (IFPRI). http://www.ifpri.org/sites/default/files/publications/massp pn9.pdf

Mutangadura, G.B. (2005) 'Gender, HIV/AIDS and rural livelihoods in southern Africa: addressing the challenges', *JENDA: A Journal of Culture and African Women Studies*, Issue 7.

Nambote, M.A. (1998) 'Agricultural Extension Policy in Malawi: Past experiences and future directions' in Ahmed, A.G.M. and Mlay, W. eds. *Environment and Sustainable Development in Eastern and Southern Africa: Some critical issues.* Houndmills: MacMillan Press Limited in Association with OSSREA.

Narotzky, S. (1997) *New Directions in Economic Anthropology*, London: Pluto Press.

National Statistical Office (NSO), (2002). 1998 Malawi Population and Housing Census, Analytical Report, Zomba, Malawi

Natter, W. and Jones III, J.P. (1997) 'Space and other uncertainties', in Benko, G. and Strohmayer, U. (eds.), *Space and Social Theory: Interpreting modernity and postmodernity.* Oxford: Blackwell.

Nayaran, D. (1997), *Voices of the Poor, Poverty and Social Capital in Tanzania*, Washington DC: World Bank.

Nyamnjoh, F.B., 2000, 'For Many are Called but Few are Chosen': Globalization and Popular Disenchantment in Africa', in *African Sociological Review*, 4 (2), 2000, pp. 1- 45.

Nyamnjoh, F.B. (2002) 'A child is one person's only in the womb': domestication, agency and subjectivity in the Cameroonian grassfields', in Werbner, R. (ed) *Postcolonial Subjectivities in Africa*, and London: Zed Books. Pp 111-138.

Nyamnjoh, F.B. (2005) 'Fishing in troubled waters: disquettes and thiofs in Dakar', *Africa* 75 (3), 295 – 324.

Nyamnjoh F.B and Jimu, I.M. (2005) 'Success or Failure of Developmental States in Africa: Exploration of the Development Experiences in a Global Context' in Mbabazi, P and Taylor, I. (eds.) *The African Developmental State? Lessons from Botswana and Uganda.* Dakar: CODESRIA.

Oakley, P. and Marsden, D. (1984), *Approaches to Participation in Rural Development*, Geneva: International Labour Office.

Olsson, J. and Wohlgemuth, L. (eds) (2003) 'Dialogue in pursuit of development – an introduction', *Dialogue in Pursuit of Development.* Stockholm: Edita Norstedts Tryckeri AB.

Orr, a and Orr, S. (2002) Agricultural and Micro Enterprise in Malawi's Rural South. ODI Agricultural Research and Extension Network. Network Paper No. 119. January 2002.

Page, B., 2002, 'Accumulation by dispossession: communities and water privatisation in Cameroon'. PRINWASS First International Conference on the theme 'Meaningful Interdisciplinarity' Challenges and Opportunities for Water Research' School of Geography and the Environment, University of Oxford, April 24-25, 2002.

Pahl, R. (1995) 'Friendly society', *New Statesman Society* 10:3:95.

Pearson, R. (2000), 'Rethinking gender matters in development', in Allen, T. and Thomas, A. (eds.) Poverty *and Development into the 21st Century*. Oxford: The Open University in Association with Oxford University Press.

Pellekaan, J.W.H. and Hartnett, T. (2000), 'Poverty in sub-Saharan Africa: Causes and characteristics', in *Overcoming Rural Poverty in Africa*, Proceedings of the workshop, Accelerating Rural Development in Africa: Towards a Political Commitment to Break the Cycle of Poverty, held at Airlie House, Virginia USA September 22-24, 1996.

Phiri, K.M. (2001) History and the Past, Present and Future of Black People. Inaugural lecture delivered on 14 September, 2001, at the University Great Hall, Zomba, Malawi.

Post, J. (1996), *Space For Small Enterprises: reflections on urban livelihood and planning in the Sudan*, Amsterdam: Thesis Publishers.

Pryor, F.C. (1990) *The political economy of poverty, equity and growth: Malawi and Madagascar*. Oxford, United Kingdom: Oxford University Press.

Rahman, A. (1993), *People's Self-development: perspectives on participatory action research a journey through experience*, Dhaka: Mohiuddin Ahmed, The University Press.

Reardon, T., J. Berdegué, and G. Escobar (2001). 'Rural Nonfarm Employment and Incomes in Latin America: Overview and Policy Implications.' World Development, Vol. 29, No. 3, pp. 395-409.

Rodney, W. (1973) How Europe Underdeveloped Africa. London: Bogle-L'Ouverture Publications and Dar-es-Salaam: Tanzanian Publishing House.

Rogerson, C.M. and D.M. Hart (1989) 'The struggle for the streets: deregulation and hawking in South Africa's major urban areas', in *Social Dynamics, A Journal of Centre for African Studies* 15 (1) Pp 29-45.

Rogerson, C.M. and Beavon, K.S.O. (1985), 'A tradition of repression: the street traders of Johannesburg', in Bromley, R. (ed) *Planning for Small Enterprises in Third World Cities*, Oxford: Pergamon Press. Pp 233 – 245.

Rweyemamu, J.F. (1992) *Third World Options: Power, security and the hope for another development*. Dar es Salaam: Tanzania Publishing House.

Sahlins M (1974) *Stone Age Economics*, London: Tavistock Publications Ltd.

Saith, A. (1992) *The Rural Non-Farm Economy: Processes and Policies*, Geneva: International Labour Office.

Salvatore, D. and Dowling, E.T. (1977) *Development Economics*, New York: McGraw Book Company.

Sandbrook, R. (1982) *The Politics of Basic Needs: Urban aspects of assaulting poverty in Africa*. London: Heinemann.

Schejtman, A. (1999) 'Urban dimensions in rural development', *Cepal Review* 67, pp. 15 – 32.

Scoones, I. (1998) *Sustainable Livelihoods: A framework for analysis.* IDS Working Paper 72.

Scoones I and Wolmer W. (2003) 'Challenges for rural development in southern Africa', *IDS Bulletin* Vol. 34 No 3 2003, pp 1-14.

Scoones I. (2009) 'Livelihoods perspectives and rural development', *Journal of Peasant Studies* 36 (1). ISSN 0306-6150 print/ISSN 1743-9361 online. (accessed on 9 November 2010). http://www.tandf.co.uk/journals/pdf/papers/FJPS_36_1_2009.pdf

Seers, D. (1969) 'The meaning of development' *International Development Review* Vol, 11, No. 4.

Shipton, P. (1992) 'Debts and trespasses: land, mortgages, and the ancestors in western Kenya', *Africa* 62 (3), 357 – 388.

Sikod, F. (2007) 'Gender division of labour and women's decision-making power in rural households in Cameroon', *Africa Development,* Vol. 32, No. 3, 2007, pp. 58–71.

Simone, A. (1998) 'Urban social fields in Africa', *Social Text* 56, 71 – 89.

Singh, K. (1999) *Rural Development: Principle, policies and management.* New Delhi: Sage Publications.

Stambuli, P.K. (2002) 'Political change, economic transition and catalysis of IMF/World Bank Economic Models- the case of Malawi.', Presented at conference on 'Malawi after Banda: perspectives in a regional African context' Centre of Commonwealth Studies, University of Stirling, Scotland, 4-5 September 2002.

Stilwell, F. (2002) *Political economy: the contents of economic ideas.* Oxford: Oxford University Press.

Streeten, P.P. (1995), *Thinking About Development*, Cambridge: Cambridge University Press.

Swift, R. (1998) 'The Cocoa Chain', *New Internationalist*, August, pp 7 – 30.

Szirmai, A. (2005) *The Dynamics of Socio-economic Development: an introduction.* Cambridge University Press.

Taylor, I. (2001) 'No mathatha (?): Botswana's strategies for Gaborone's place in the global economy' A paper presented at a conference 'State/ Society responses to Globalisation: Case studies from Japan and Southern Africa' Stellenbosch, South Africa August 2 – 3, 2001.

Tellegen, N. (1997) *Rural Enterprises in Malawi: Necessity or opportunity?* Aldershot, Hampshire: Ashgate Publishing Limited.

Thomas, B.P. (1985), *Politics, Participation and Poverty: Development Through Self-help in Kenya*, Boulder: Westview Press, Inc.

Todaro, M.P. (1992), *Economics for a Developing World: an introduction to principles, problems and policies for development.* London: Longman.

Tripp, A.M. (1997) *Challenging the Rules: The Politics of Liberalization and the Urban Informal Economy in Tanzania.* Berkeley: University of California Press.

Ubink, J. (2006) 'Land, chiefs and custom in peri-urban Ghana', Paper for the International Conference on 'Land, Poverty, Social Justice and Development', organized by ISS and ICCO, 12-14 January 2006, The Hague, The Netherlands.

www.iss.nl/content/download/3624/35301/file/Ubink.p df (accessed 22 September 2010)

Ubink, J.M. (2008) 'Negotiated or negated? the rhetoric and reality of customary tenure in an Ashanti village in Ghana', *Africa* 78 (2), 264 – 287.

United Nations Conference on Trade and Development (UNCTAD) (2001) *Economic Development in Africa: Performance, Prospects and Policy Issues*. New York and Geneva: United Nations

University of Malawi (2012) *UNIMA Strategic Plan 2012 – 2017*. Zomba: University of Malawi.

Valdivia, C and Quiroz, R (2001) 'Rural livelihood strategies, assets and economic portfolios in coping with climatic perturbations: a case study of the Bolivian Andes', Paper presented at the Social Organization and Land Management Session, Integrated Natural Resource Management for Sustainable Agriculture, Forestry and Fisheries, 28-31 August, CIAT, Cali Colombia.

Vannini, P. (ed) (2009b) 'Material culture studies and the sociology and anthropology of technology', in *Material Culture and technology in Everyday Life: ethnographic approaches*, pp. 15 - 26. New York: Peter Lang.

Vele, M. (1978) 'Rural villages and peri-urban settlement: a case-study of circulation from the central province', Institute of Applies Social and Economic Research (IASER) Occasional Paper, Number 2. Papua New Guinea.

Vyasulu, V. 2002) 'Development and Participation: what is missing? ', *Economic and Political Weekly*, 37 (28): 2869-2871.

Wandschneider, T. (2003) 'Determinants of access to rural non-farm employment: Evidence from Africa, South Asia and transition economies' Natural Resources Institute NRI Report No. 2758.

Wandschneider, T and Junior R. D. (2003) Rural Non-Farm Economy Best practice and strategies for promoting rural non-farm employment through project interventions NRI Report No: 2756

Warburton, P (1990) 'Appropriate Technology' in Ross, S. (editor) *Longman Coordinated Geography*, Harlow, Essex: Longman Group (UK) Limited. (p. 76-77).

Warburton, D., 1998, 'A passionate dialogue: community and sustainable development', in Warburton, D. (ed) *Community and Sustainable Development*, London: Earthscan Publishing Ltd.

Watts, E.R. (1969) *New Hope for Rural Africa*. Nairobi: African Publishing House.

Whiteside, M. (1998) 'When the whole is more than the sum of the parts- the effect of cross-border interactions on livelihood security in southern Malawi and northern Mozambique', A Report for Oxfam GB. http://www.eldis.org/fulltext/malmoz.pdf (accessed 14 March 2009)

Wilk R.R. (1996) *Economies and Cultures: Foundations of economic anthropology*, Oxford: Westview Press.

Williams, G. (1982) 'Taking the part of peasants', in Harriss, J.(ed.) *Rural Development: theories of peasant economy and agrarian change,* London: Hutchinson (Publishers) Ltd.

Wilson, G. (1990) 'Technology in development' in Allen, T and Thomas, A. (ed.) *Poverty and Development in the 1990s.* Oxford University Press in Association

Woodson, D.C. (2007) 'What do indicators indicate? Reflections on the trial and tribulations of using food aid to promote development in Haiti', in Field, L.W. and Fox, R.G. (eds) *Anthropology Put to Work*, Oxford: Berg. Pp 129-147.

World Bank, (1988), *Rural Development: World Bank Experience 1965-1986*, Washington DC: World Bank.

World Bank, (1990) *World Development Report*, New York: Oxford University Press.

World Bank (2000), *World Development Report 2000/2001: Attacking Poverty*, New York: Oxford University Press.

World Bank (2002) *World Development Report: Building Institutions for Markets.* Oxford University Press.

World Bank (2006) *Malawi Poverty and Vulnerability Assessment: investing in our future.* Washington DC: World Bank.

World Commission of Environment and Development (1987) *Our Common Future.* Oxford: University Press.

Worpole, K. and Greenhalgh, L., 1996, The Freedom of The City, London: Demos.

Yaro, J.A. 'Is deagrarianisation real? A study of livelihood activities in rural northern Ghana' *The Journal of Modern African Studies* (2006), 44:1:125-156.

Youdeowei, A. and Akinwumi, J.A. (1986), 'Agricultural Development, Land Tenure and Cooperatives', in Youdewei, A., Zedinma, E. and Onazi, O.C. (eds.), *Introduction to Tropical Agriculture*, London: Longman.

Zoomers, A. (1999) *Linking Livelihood Strategies to Development: Experiences from the Bolivia Andes.* Amsterdam: Royal Tropical Institute.

Zoomers, A. (2010) 'Globalisation and the foreignisation of space: seven processes driving the current global land grab', *The Journal of Peasant Studies* 37 (2), 429 – 447.

Printed in the United States
By Bookmasters